DR. RICHARD FURMAN'S SAVE YOUR LIFE CHOLESTEROL PLAN

BERKLEY BOOKS, NEW YORK

Unless otherwise noted, Scripture quotations are from *The New King James Version.* Copyright © 1979, 1980, 1982, Thomas Nelson, Inc., Publishers.

This Berkley book contains the complete text of the original hardcover version.

DR. RICHARD FURMAN'S SAVE YOUR LIFE CHOLESTEROL PLAN

A Berkley Book / published by arrangement with Thomas Nelson, Inc., Publishers

PRINTING HISTORY
Thomas Nelson edition published 1990
Berkley edition / May 1991

A BERKLEY BOOK ® TM 757,375
Berkley Books are published by The Berkley Publishing Group, 200 Madison Avenue, New York, New York 10016. The name "BERKLEY" and the "B" logo are trademarks belonging to Berkley Publishing Corporation.

PRINTED IN THE UNITED STATES OF AMERICA

10 9 8 7 6 5

To the memory of the 600,000 Americans who die from heart attacks each year. They didn't plan to kill themselves prematurely; they simply didn't plan <u>not</u> to do it.

To the memory of the 18 percent whose first symptom of heart disease is death.

To those who survive their first heart attack or chest pain.

To those who desire to be as fit at age forty-nine as they were at age nineteen.

To those who realize that it's not so much how long you live that is so important, but what type of health you can enjoy after reaching the fifty-year milestone.

To those who are striving to reach their full potential in life, who want to look younger and live longer.

To those who want to enhance weight loss and prevent coronary heart disease, who want to cut through the confusion of "good" and "bad" cholesterol and follow an aggressive action plan to thwart the number one killer in America, the silent killer called cholesterol.

To you, the readers, who want the best life has to offer, who are willing to visualize your bodies as your most prized possessions. I challenge you not only to read these pages but to study them; review them until you completely understand the diseases that would have probably caused your demise. I challenge you to reach your optimum weight, to develop your physical condition to peak performance. I challenge you to engrain this Save Your Life Cholesterol Plan into your life and become the healthiest possible you. Health once gone is sought forever!

CONTENTS

AMERICAN MEDICAL ASSOCIATION

535 NORTH DEARBORN STREET • CHICAGO, ILLINOIS 60610
PHONE (312) 645-5000 • Fax (312) 645-4184 • Telex 28-0248

PRESIDENT

JAMES E. DAVIS, M.D.
2609 N. Duke Street
Suite 402
Durham, North Carolina 27704

Americans today are more health conscious and health involved than ever before. We know that we can improve our health and prevent many illnesses by what we do for ourselves, and that we have an obligation to ourselves to do so.

Most Americans today know that heart disease is the number one killer of both men and women and that a heart attack happens after months and years when the arteries to our hearts silently, and without warning, get plugged with cholesterol. We are learning that we can help prevent the cholesterol syndrome from developing by eating the proper foods, exercising, maintaining normal blood pressure, and avoiding tobacco.

Dr. Richard Furman is a skilled surgeon who helps people by operating on clogged arteries. However, he is driven by the fact that he can prolong more lives and save more lives by educating people about cholesterol and its associated problems than by operating on arteries already closing down. This book, truly a labor of love and dedication, is written in clear, easily understood language for general use by the public. At the same time physicians, medical students, and all of us involved in advising patients or providing health care will find it an invaluable tool. It is factual, authoritative, and supported by an exhaustive review of the medical literature.

At the time when Americans are seeking and need more information in order to help themselves, when the American Medical Association, the American Heart Association, and innumerable other national groups are waging wars and campaigns against cholesterol and for a better and longer life for all Americans, this work will be widely received, used and appreciated.

James E. Davis

PREFACE

Years ago an aging, free-spirited comedian said that if he had known he was going to live so long, he would have taken much better care of his body. As we rush pell-mell into the twenty-first century, this statement is being made by millions of Americans—and well it should be. Our life span today is longer than it has ever been, and there are many highly qualified physicians who believe that a ninety-plus-year life span will soon be the norm. This could be immensely exciting and rewarding or it could bring on problems beyond calculation if our physical health deteriorates. Obviously, the best time to protect your health is while you still have it. That's the reason *Dr. Richard Furman's Save Your Life Cholesterol Plan* is a book whose time has come.

Dr. Richard Furman has given us a "medical" book in non-medical language. He has written it in a style that would be the envy of any mystery writer or novelist, as far as creating excitement and interest are concerned. The book involves you personally from "hello" to "good-bye." He creates a relationship between patient and physician that is open, honest, informative, and motivating.

For the past sixteen years, I've personally been very much interested in and concerned about my health and have maintained a sensible weight program through diet and exercise that has given me considerably more energy. However, I have always had to do my share of halo-adjusting as I "toughed it out" and felt just a touch of martyrdom as I did my bit about "pushing away from the table" and declining certain foods that have a universal appeal but add cholesterol *and* pounds. (My body retains ice cream!)

After reading my prepublication copy of Dr. Richard Furman's *Save Your Life Cholesterol Plan*, I have taken off my halo, abandoned my call to martyrdom, and am happier and healthier than ever. For the first time, I know that by following Dr. Furman's program with his wide selection of delicious, less expensive, more nutritious foods, and sensible health care procedures, I can maintain the proper weight and have a higher energy level without getting hungry. Now, *that* is exciting!

One of the most significant benefits of incorporating Dr. Furman's recommendations into our lifestyle is the effect it can have on our success in the physical, mental, and spiritual aspects of life. That could be important to everyone, but for many it could well mean the difference in providing the financial necessities as well as developing the energy required for supplying the emotional and spiritual needs of a family.

Dr. Richard Furman's *Save Your Life Cholesterol Plan* can literally save thousands of dollars in medical expenses by the adoption of these eating and exercise procedures. I encourage you to carefully read and keep on your nightstand this marvelous book as an ongoing reference. I'm convinced that if you do, I'LL SEE YOU AT THE TOP—in good shape!

Zig Ziglar

Zig Ziglar

DR. RICHARD FURMAN'S SAVE YOUR LIFE CHOLESTEROL PLAN

1
_____

GOALS AND COMMITMENT: THE KEYS TO SUCCESSFUL DIETING

The Wilsons both knew they were overweight. Evelyn was sixteen pounds overweight, and Andy was carrying forty extra pounds. They had tried different ways to lose, sometimes on separate diets and sometimes together. Many times they were successful; but they always put the weight back on after the excitement of losing it wore off. Evelyn dreaded putting on a swimsuit, and Andy didn't like the way he hung over his belt buckle. As a matter of fact, he had quit wearing knit shirts.

She had a friend who was at least eighty pounds overweight, and Evelyn didn't see herself as being all that fat. Yet, she often wished she was as trim as when she finished college and got married. Somehow she just hadn't lost all the weight she gained after each of her children was born. She had gained eight to ten pounds with each child and lost most of it within six months, but not all. Actually, one way to look at it is to say that her sixteen pounds is the accumulation of less than an extra one-half slice of bread a day for the fifteen years she has been married. Whatever the reason, she wanted to be trim again.

Andy was definitely considered fat, even by American standards. He knew he was overweight but didn't consider himself significantly obese. It had happened so insidiously. Until he was about thirty he had played basketball in a church league, but then he started spending more time on the job and spending less time on sports or exercise. His waistline had slowly increased over eight inches during the past seven years. At first, he asked his wife to let the waist of his pants out a bit. Finally, he started buying the next larger size pants whenever he needed a new pair. No big deal, just the aging process. It wasn't that noticeable to him or his friends. It was sort of like the beach eroding from one summer vacation to the next. You barely noticed it, and it didn't make that much difference to him.

He was eating no more than he did when he married fifteen years ago, but two changes accounted for his weight gain. He used to participate in sports year-round. He was still eating the same, but he had quit exercising. Second, he had developed the habit of drinking a little beer or wine almost every day. He could control the amount of alcohol, but he realized it was excess calories.

He had never thought much about being overweight until a friend made a small comment that brought him to see himself as others did. His friend made a little joke about being heavy around the middle. For the first time in his life, Andy decided he really wanted to be trim again. He knew four out of five people who lose weight eventually regain it. He had been one of those four many times.

He had heard about a group of people on a diet called the Save Your Life Cholesterol Plan. He was told it was a *guaranteed* plan—guaranteed that he would lose the weight and guaranteed that he would keep it off. The plan stressed there were no gimmicks, no crash programs, and no unusual diets that would be impossible to follow for long periods. The plan emphasized a permanent solution to their weight problems.

The theme of the Save Your Life Cholesterol Plan was that permanent weight control by the diet taught today was the same diet to be used a year later, which was the same diet they would be on for the rest of their lives. The plan wasn't really a diet but a new eating-habit development program. He decided to talk to his wife about joining the plan.

"The people I have talked to swear by it," he told Evelyn. "It makes sense. The plan is put on by a group of doctors. You visit each of five or six doctors, and each one tells you one aspect of the diet program. Supposedly, when you finish visiting all the doctors, you will understand all the necessities of losing the weight and a medically sound way to keep it off."

"I'm ready to try anything." Evelyn really perked up. Her husband was telling her how she might reach that dream she had had for the past five years about losing her excess weight once and for all. "Can you get us both appointments?"

On the day of their first appointment they were invited into Dr. William Franklin's office. He had an assuring manner and welcomed them with as much enthusiasm as anyone they had ever met.

"Have a seat and we'll get right down to the business of developing the type of body you desire to have." He was already planting key words in their minds: *developing* and *desire*. He also had them sit together on a love seat that was barely big enough for the two of them together. He wanted them to feel a little uncomfortable because of the excess weight each was carrying.

"You both want to lose weight. That is the primary reason you're here. That's fine, but we want to teach you not only how to lose weight but also how cholesterol and weight loss are related. A low-cholesterol diet is still anathema to most Americans. As a whole, we still favor the steaks, cheese, eggs, and butter. We've been reared this way; we don't know any better. This attitude leads to the cholesterol syndrome, and that is quickly leading to the physical downfall of America."

"What's the cholesterol syndrome?" Evelyn asked.

"You hear a lot about cigarettes and smoking causing lung cancer. Rightly so, because smoking is responsible for the deaths of 500,000 Americans yearly from chronic lung disease, emphysema, arterial disease, stomach problems, and bronchial problems. Over 100,000 die from lung cancer alone. The New York Medical Association reported that 14 to 16 percent of all deaths each year in America are the direct result of smoking. We have passed a law that the Surgeon General's warning about the correlation of smoking and lung cancer must be placed on cigarette packs. We make a big fuss over these 100,000 deaths, and rightly so because each life is valuable.

■ More people die from coronary artery disease than from all forms of cancer combined. What you eat can be worse than having cancer.

"In contrast, we don't see much warning about the causal relationship of cholesterol and coronary heart disease. This disease of the arteries of the heart is responsible for more than 550,000 deaths in the United States every year. Coronary heart disease is responsible for more deaths than all forms of cancer combined. Coronary heart disease is caused by atherosclerosis, a slowly progressive disease in which cholesterol is silently laid down in the walls of the arteries of the heart until they are choked and occluded. The process begins early in life but rarely produces any symptoms until middle or late life. Many times, it goes undetected until an individual feels the anguish and pain of a heart attack. This first attack often is fatal: the cholesterol syndrome has gone unnoticed and unannounced until it makes its fatal lunge at the unknowing victim, much like a prowling lion attacks a grazing wildebeest without any warning. Life ends quickly without the first indication that anything is wrong. The Save Your Life Cholesterol Plan is that warning.

"AIDS has taken the limelight in the media covering dreaded deadly diseases. The AIDS death rate is on the rise and is indeed significant. However, over the past several years, seventy times as many people have lost their lives because of their teeth . . . they have been eating wrongly. They haven't done anything morally wrong. Most victims of coronary heart disease are innocent of any crime. They were simply ignorant of the cholesterol syndrome.

"The cholesterol syndrome is the combination of physiological effects that lead to the occlusion of the coronary arteries by cholesterol deposited within their walls. The syndrome begins with the eating of cholesterol; then that particle of cholesterol is coated by fatty proteins in the body, carried through the blood, and pounded into the walls of the arteries. The cholesterol syndrome is an exciting one to learn about. It is simple and easy to understand. Knowledge of this syndrome will help prolong your life, lose weight, and avoid that number one killer in America we just discussed.

"The cholesterol syndrome is the culmination of the present American life-style of eating habits, which is the pathway we travel every time we eat an average American meal. The final step in this syndrome is death. That happens when enough cholesterol is deposited into the walls of the arteries in the heart to cause complete occlusion and stop the vital blood flow to the heart muscles.

"We want to show you how to change your eating habits through the Save Your Life Cholesterol Plan. We want to put a warning label on some of the foods you eat. We want our diet plan to become the accepted eating pattern in America. We want to trim that 550,000-a-year death rate to a much lower level. It's a shame to have Americans so educated about the warning signs of cancer, yet so ignorant of a disease that leads to such a greater number of deaths than cancer. We want to teach you the detailed anatomy of the cholesterol syndrome. We want to help prolong your life, not just lose weight.

"What the Save Your Life Cholesterol Plan teaches will be factual and medically sound. Our plan is based on medical studies as published in articles in the leading medical journals. We will furnish you with these references for further study. However, our basic plan is for the layman, the average steak-and-hamburger-eating citizen. No part of the cholesterol syndrome will be beyond your understanding. By the time you finish this plan, you will be at your proper weight, active, and eating a nourishing diet you will enjoy. You will like it because it is making you feel great. You will be in better physical condition than you have been since high school. You're going to be in the shape you need to ensure reaching your full potential in life. Our aim is to make you the best you can be.

"I think my part of the Save Your Life Cholesterol Plan is the most important aspect of the whole program," Dr. Franklin continued. "If you don't succeed with this part, the rest is doomed to fail. I base my entire instructions on a verse found in the Old Testament. Proverbs 23:7 reads, 'For as he thinks in his heart, so is he.' That's what my session with you is all about. I want you first to decide in your heart that you are going to succeed in the Save Your Life Cholesterol Plan, and then we'll develop it for you. First in the mind, then in action. You have to develop the *desire* to lose weight; come up with a real reason to become thin—whatever it may be. Do not begin your diet until this desire is firmly fixed in your mind or you will not be successful."

"Oh, I've wanted to lose weight before," Evelyn interrupted. "Really wanted to more than most anything else."

"I am not talking about wanting to," replied Dr. Franklin. "What I am talking about goes much deeper than *wants*. To reach a certain weight, to develop a certain appearance, has to become such a goal that losing weight burns in your mind. You have to develop an excitement if success is to follow. Your desire to lose weight has to be the first thing you think of in the morning and the last you think of at night. You have to be convinced in your mind that you are going to accomplish the goal."

"But how do you ever build yourself up to something like that?" Evelyn was a little set back that her *wants* had not been good enough for her to succeed in the past. "I've never set a goal like that in my life—much less accomplished it in my mind before I started working on it in reality."

"The actual losing of the weight will be the easy part," Dr. Franklin informed her. "Convincing yourself to do it and determining that you are going to do it are the hard parts. That's what I want to teach you and your husband today—the hardest part, and the most important determining factor of our program. You have to learn the importance of goal-setting and how to apply it to losing weight or your weight will fluctuate the rest of your life."

"Okay." Andy was becoming interested in this aspect of the diet. He had not given much thought before to setting the goal for losing weight, but if the doctor thought it was that important, he'd go along with his advice. "You mentioned coming up with convincing reasons for losing weight. Tell me how to convince myself that I really need to lose it."

Dr. Franklin turned that question back toward Andy. "You are forty pounds overweight. Do you realize how much more work that puts on your heart? Do you know how hard it would be if you put a forty-pound rock in a little red wagon and pulled it around behind you all day?" He looked at Evelyn. "Or a sixteen-pound rock for that matter? Not only would you have to work harder to do it, but imagine that your heart is connected to that rock with some tubing and has to pump blood into that rock all day and night. Think of the extra work load on the heart that would entail. Added to all that, you have the increased risk of high blood pressure, stroke, and heart attack, and you have all kinds of good reasons to lose weight."

"You're saying that overall good health is the reason to lose our extra weight we're carrying around?" asked Evelyn.

"That should be reason in itself," responded Dr. Franklin, "but most people need something very personal that tips the scales—no pun intended—for them finally to decide they are going to do it."

"What do you mean, *personal?*" asked Andy.

■ *Weight loss in itself may be the only problem you need to correct to bring your cholesterol to a normal count. Commit to a normal weight.*

"Well, it could be something big like your spouse decides to leave you and you realize it's partially because you're over-weight." Dr. Franklin began to mention a few reasons that other patients had decided to lose weight. "Or it could be something insignificant like meeting a friend you haven't seen in years and the person telling you, without really thinking, that you have gained weight. It could be looking in the mirror and real-izing you either have to lose weight or get bigger clothes. Sometimes, it simply is the realization that the only thing be-tween your weight today and the day you graduated from col-lege is your desire to become once again the beautiful woman you were then, with a few years of maturity thrown in." He glanced at Evelyn with a smile.

"Do you mean I really could wear a size seven again?"

"First in the mind, then in actuality." Dr. Franklin reassured her that she could actually accomplish her goal if she were just willing to pay the price. "Now, you both need the ammunition to fight the battle."

"You have us ready," responded Andy as he opened the note-pad the doctor gave them.

"COMMITMENT," Dr. Franklin began. "Write it down. The first step is commitment. You have to commit to this plan of losing weight. Do you know what commitment means? It means that you sell out to the idea—for whatever reason you decide on; but you sell out completely to the idea of losing weight and keeping it off. You have to decide you want it off more than anything else; you are willing to do everything possible. Then you will succeed, but only if you are willing to commit to following the plan closely."

"What's the first step? After commitment, that is." Andy was anxious to hear what the doctor had to say.

"After committing to lose weight, you have to set your goal." Dr. Franklin began to emphasize what is so important to the Save Your Life Cholesterol Plan eating habits that the couple would have to develop.

"I've set goals before to lose weight, but it didn't seem to help that much," Andy responded.

"Everyone is born with the necessary elements to succeed," the doctor began. "You have within you right now everything it takes to make you successful in losing the weight you need to lose. It is similar to digging an oil well on land many consider worthless. The oil is there underneath, hidden all the while. It just takes someone who's committed to drilling for the oil to get a geyser. I'm telling you, you already have the ingredients within you to succeed in losing your weight. We just have to teach you how to drill for the oil.

"What is the one thing that will cause these built-in values to come forth and be put to use? What one thing will pull the most out of you, and prime you to do your very best in how you go about losing your weight? The answer to those questions is one word: GOALS.

"I hate to see obese men or women in their forties or fifties who realize how different their lives could have been if they had just lost weight years before. They become might-have-beens, the men or women who never lived up to what they could have become. They had it in them to change their eating styles, but they never discovered the secret of bringing out the best. They were made to run like the wind but ended up crawling along like a snail, never discovering what life could have been like. They could have been sitting in first class but flew economy fare simply because they set no goals."

Dr. Franklin looked directly at Andy and Evelyn and paused to emphasize what he was about to say. "You ask how important are goals? A person's goal is everything! It is the difference between success and failure in your diet program. Without it, you will float aimlessly up and down the weight chart. With it, you will have a singleness of mind, a direction, a motivating factor that will see you to the end and then help you persist in your major objective of good health. Your goals are the oil derrick, the pipeline, and the drill to reach the Spindletop buried deep within you."

"Well, I thought I had set goals before, but maybe not the way you're speaking about them," Andy said.

"Have you really set goals to lose weight, or have you simply had a desire to lose weight?" the doctor asked. "There is a vast difference in simply wanting something and committing to a goal concerning the same circumstance.

"No, I would say you have never set a goal to lose weight before, not the kind I'm talking about. The type of goal I'm speaking of becomes your life-style. You breathe it, you sleep it, you live it until it becomes habit. Once the road toward that goal becomes habit, you've got it won. This should be one of the most rigorous goals you've ever set for yourself. It's one that will change your life." Dr. Franklin didn't let up on his point. "Once you develop the habit of losing weight, which will take about a month, you will continue that habit until you reach your goal."

"Okay, so we set a goal to lose some weight, and we reach that goal," Andy edged in. "How do we keep the weight off?"

"Habits culminate in life-style." Dr. Franklin didn't change his pace. "By the time you reach your goal, you will have developed a completely new style of eating. The eating habits we teach you to lose weight with will be the same eating habits you will use to maintain your weight at that desired level. You will simply be able to eat a larger quantity of the same foods later on. We'll get into the details of that later. Right now, let's talk about conquering your old eating habits in your mind."

"You mean I won't crave Snickers candy bars and Oreos by the dozen with a big glass of milk just before I go to bed?" Andy was partly joking.

"Exactly," responded Dr. Franklin. "You will slowly lose that craving. Oh, you may eat some of those every once in a while, but the day will come when you can take them or leave them.

"But before this can happen, there is still something you must do in preparation for setting your goals," the doctor instructed. "Before you set your goal for what you want to weigh, you have to develop the desire in your heart to such a degree that absolutely nothing can come to block your path."

"What do you mean, *develop the desire?*" asked Evelyn. "How do you develop something as abstract as desire? Desire isn't a skill that can be developed, is it?"

"You're correct in one sense. Desire is a quality, but developing that desire is a skill I want you to learn. You have to tell yourself that you mean business, that you're tough, confident, bold. You have to sell yourself on the reality that you are going to do it."

"How do you do that?" Evelyn wanted to know.

"I'll use a recent patient of mine to illustrate developing desire and show you how important it is to be convinced in your mind that you mean business. This gentleman had coughed some blood out of his lungs. After a thorough workup, including a bronchoscopy to actually see into the air passages in his lungs, all I could find was an area of irritation in the middle air passage of his right lung. It wasn't cancer, but he had damaged the lining of that part of his lung. He had to quit smoking, and I told him so.

"Two weeks later he returned for a follow-up visit. He had not quit smoking but had 'cut way down,' he said. I told him that he was not going to quit smoking by cutting down, that it was even worse for him to cut down; he was only kidding himself, thinking he was in the act of quitting. I explained that it would be better for him to continue smoking full-speed ahead; then I would still have a crack at convincing him to quit. As long as he was cutting down, he would not listen to more advice. I convinced him of the need to completely convict his own mind that he had to quit smoking for good. He accepted my philosophy.

■ *Setting goals is the difference in what-might-have-been and success.*

"Three weeks later he sat in my office telling me he went out and bought a carton of cigarettes and placed packs of them all through his house and in his car. Every time he saw the cigarettes and refused them, he was reinforcing his mind with the truth that he had actually quit smoking. He did not quit smoking until the day he convinced himself that he meant business. He became tough with himself, decisive, absolute, firm. He succeeded. So can you.

"Now, I'm going to teach you how to develop desire. The first action is to write it down. Put your thoughts in writing. Organize them to state your goal concerning your weight and put it on paper. Make it specific and concise and definite. Place this goal where you can see it. Type it up and tape it to your scales. Look at it every morning when you step on those scales just to prove to yourself you mean business. Make your mind hear you. Make it hear that you are serious in this matter, just like my patient placed packs of cigarettes all over his house."

Evelyn interrupted. "It will be easy to decide my goal. I remember what I weighed when I got married, two babies ago. That's going to be my goal."

"Good," Dr. Franklin responded. "That takes us to another means of developing that desire I was talking about. I've told you to tell your mind your goal, to talk to your mind's ear. Now, I want you to convince your mind's eye of your goal."

"How?" Evelyn wanted to know.

"By starting to see your goal already completed. Begin to see yourself as already having lost the weight," he instructed her.

"I like that picture," Andy interrupted. "I do look good with forty pounds off. I'm liking this already."

"I'm going to show you how to be successful with that goal," Dr. Franklin added, "how to make that picture in your mind become a reality. I want to show you both how to become successful at losing weight."

"You mean after I achieve that goal?" Andy asked.

"No, I mean when you eat one bite less of your food, when you lose that first pound. You see, success is not realized when you finally lose that fortieth pound. Success is a progression, not an end point. Once you make the commitment, set the goal, and start to work on it, you are a success. Whether anyone else considers you a success is of no concern. Success is each ounce lost, each mouthful not taken.

"In my own mind, I became successful in becoming a doctor that first day of medical school. I had set my goal to complete medical school and become a doctor. As soon as I actively started working on that goal, I became successful at it. I did not become a doctor on the day of graduation. No, I became a doctor one day at a time all the way through school."

"So, you mean I don't have to wait until I lose the whole

forty pounds to feel good about myself? I can look at myself as a successful dieter right away?" Andy already had good insight into the whole process of developing a new life-style of eating, beginning right then.

"Exactly," Dr. Franklin agreed. "And it is important to see yourself in that light. It will affect your whole life. It will change your outlook on everything around you—your relationship with your wife, your work, your reactions to friends. All because you will have convinced your mind and you will know deep in your heart that you are going to really reach that goal."

"That's exciting!" Evelyn had been taking it all in, writing notes as fast as she could. She looked at Dr. Franklin. "What else do we need to know about goals?"

"You need to know the structure of goal-setting," he continued.

"You mean there's a certain structure to follow?" Andy asked. "I'm not so sure I can ever become as organized as you on these weight goals. Are you that organized in everything you do?"

"Not with everything, but I do know how to organize a goal and get it done," the doctor replied.

"Well, go ahead and tell us. Our pencils are sharpened," Andy stated.

"You each have to take those weight goals and break them down into workable units," the doctor began.

"For simplicity's sake, let's work on the forty-pound goal and apply what I say to that." Dr. Franklin nodded at Andy. "Let's call your forty-pound loss your major goal."

"Makes sense," Andy responded.

"Next, let's say you want to lose ten pounds the first month." The doctor began his breakdown.

"Oh, I've done that before," Andy laughed. "I call it 'crash diet number one.' I crash and burn. I lose ten pounds in two weeks. Takes me four weeks to gain it back. Gaining back is one thing I do successfully."

"You'll lose the ten pounds," Dr. Franklin assured him. "But you won't gain it back. Not only will I guarantee you won't gain it back, but I guarantee you—you'll lose another ten, and another ten, and another ten; and finally, I guarantee that you will never gain it back."

"Just how can you be so confident, doctor?" Evelyn asked. "You don't know how many diets he's been on before. You don't know how bad our track records really are."

■ *Change your life-style of eating—your only hope for permanent weight control!*

"I don't really care about the past. The one thing I do is strive toward our present goal," the doctor explained. "Forget the past; we work in the *right now* time zone. Just as Paul said in the New Testament when he was reminded of past failures: 'One thing I do, forgetting those things which are behind and reaching forward to those things which are ahead, I press toward the goal . . .'

"I want you to learn to forget the past and press toward your major goal."

"Okay," Andy agreed. "So, where does the first ten pounds fit in my goal structure?"

"Each ten pounds becomes an intermediate goal," Dr. Franklin replied. He looked at Evelyn. "Or in your case, each two pounds becomes an intermediate goal. There is no time limit."

"No time limit?" Andy asked.

"Individually you do set time limits, but each person is different. I will not give you a time schedule. Both of you will develop diet plans, but each person sets his own caloric intake level and exercise program. So the time limit of each intermediate goal is left up to you, the individual." Dr. Franklin looked at both of them.

"What's a good average?" Evelyn inquired.

"A good aggressive average with strict caloric intake and consistent exercise is around eight pounds a month." Dr. Franklin gave the first of his estimates. "We aren't interested in crashing weight off; we want a slow progression that gives you time to develop eating habits to last a lifetime. We like a consistent loss of weight, and all the while, you will be developing the life-style program so important in keeping your weight off. Remember, habits develop life-styles. We just want to teach you good habits and then watch your life-style change in the way you eat and what you eat. I lost my weight by losing one and one-fourth ounces a day for ten months. Slow, but effective.

"The first challenge you'll face will be with these intermediate goals. Many obstacles will block that road of success you're traveling. Some of these obstacles will stop you in your tracks. Some will be little pebbles that aggravate you more than anything else, but there will be some boulders so big you can't see any way around them. You may wreck your car, a family member may get sick, you may take a cruise where the food is irresistible and end up going on a food binge and gaining five pounds in a week's time. You may be so tempted one night that you hit the kitchen at ten o'clock and cram every sweet and calorie-laden piece of food you can find into your mouth." Dr. Franklin was telling it like it is. He didn't make any promises that the change in life-style eating would be easy.

"I've done that before," Andy chimed in. "Sometimes on a diet I get so hungry at night I lose my control."

"Those are the boulders I'm talking about. How you handle the boulders on the intermediate goal path determines the difference between success and failure. I want you to take the initiative to decide to be good to yourself, to be successful."

"Well, tell us how to turn those boulders into success." Andy wanted specific help. "Those were the times before when I turned into a failure. The times when I broke down were the times I would usually give up and quit, especially if I hit several of these failures—boulders as you call them—in a row. They just made me realize I didn't have what it took to lose the weight I wanted to. Sooner or later, those boulders would get me down, and I'd be off my diet for good. I'd think, *What's the use?* People will just have to take me for what I am. Once that attitude crept into my mind, it was all over."

"Good insight," Dr. Franklin commended him. "The boulder fields you have to pass through on the road of intermediate ten-pound goals killed your dream, killed your goal and, worst of all, is killing you right now by that cholesterol silently blocking the arteries in your heart. Your problem has been that you left out the one key ingredient that makes it all work, the one ingredient that makes the dough rise, the one ingredient that is key to the flavor."

"I understand what you're saying," Andy agreed. "I was missing out on one little item that made the difference between winning and losing, between losing my weight and not. You're saying I did the hard work but left out one small ingredient, and that ruined the whole outcome."

"Exactly!" Dr. Franklin had Andy right at the point he needed to be.

"Well, what is that ingredient he and I both have been leaving out?" Evelyn interrupted. "I've seen it happen to him, and it's happened to me also. I hit one of those boulders, and I'm off my diet for months. What's the key, doctor?"

"PERSISTENCE." Dr. Franklin's voice was emphatic. "The one ingredient determining success or failure is persistence. That's why your commitment to your goal must be so strong. When you hit a boulder, and you will hit many, you will persist until you can work around or over it because your commitment was more than a strong wish. If your goal was really committed to and you have convinced yourself beyond any reasonable doubt that you can reach your major goal, then no amount of boulders will keep you from successfully completing each intermediate goal. With persistence, a boulder in the path becomes a temporary delay, a detour, but not an impasse, not a complete block."

"What you're saying is that during each intermediate goal, there will be times when we will get off our diet for some reason or another." Andy summarized Dr. Franklin's thoughts.

"Right," the doctor agreed.

"And we could let that either be a failure—"

Dr. Franklin interrupted, "And stop your diet and never get back on it full swing."

"Or," Andy continued, "we could begin anew the next day and be right back on the road again."

"Correct," Dr. Franklin said. "But you don't wait until the next day to begin again, or next week, or after the weekend vacation is over. You begin again *right now!* Just as soon as you have that temporary delay toward your goal, you get back on it right away. Persist. Dog it to death until you get control of it again. The real beneficiaries in this program will be the Americans who are willing to commit to their goal and persist until they develop new diet habits."

"You mean never give up!" Andy asserted. "No matter what."

"Never give up. Keep that major goal ahead of you all the time." The doctor continued to pound away at his theme. "You already know you can reach it. Persist through the temporary defeats, and with each victory, your persistence strengthens. You become stronger and stronger until the big boulders start to crumble, becoming smaller and smaller. A life-style develops and soon you are out of the boulder field. You become a champion; you have fewer and fewer problems with the boulders, and finally you develop complete control of your eating habits. Your habits have overcome all sorts of temptations so many times that the habits override the problems. And remember what happens after you develop the eating habits you want?"

"Yes," responded Evelyn. "Those habits turn into an eating life-style, and that is what keeps the weight off."

"Without really trying," the doctor continued. "That's the nice part of this program. You develop a life-style of eating habits, and then you can forget about dieting. You will automatically eat properly without having to think about it. That is what makes this diet different from other diets. You don't simply lose weight; you work on changing your eating habits that stay with you for the rest of your life."

"Okay," Andy interrupted. "I understand the major goal and intermediate goals part of the plan. Is there more?"

■ *Tomorrow's fitness is determined today.*

"Yes, the last and most vital part of the diet goal structure." Dr. Franklin's words were strong.

"What is it?" Evelyn wanted to know.

"It's called the immediate action goal. It's the cornerstone of the entire diet plan. The IMMEDIATE ACTION you take is what determines whether the whole goal framework will hold up. It's the *right now* aspect of the goal system." Dr. Franklin emphasized the importance of the present.

"What do you mean, the *right now* aspect?" Evelyn asked.

"I can tell whether you have committed yourself to lose weight by your actions the next time you eat a bite of food," the doctor began. "It's not what you plan to do tomorrow, or next Monday, or as soon as the holidays are over that determines your success. It's what you do about your goal *right now*."

"You mean we can't wait until after dinner tonight?" Evelyn sounded almost disappointed. "This is our anniversary. We were going to eat out."

"Remember, the most important aspect of the entire goal structure is the *right now* aspect, the immediate action you take toward reaching your major goal," the doctor continued. "If you haven't convinced your mind about *right now,* today, you surely won't convince it tomorrow."

"I agree with what you're saying, but I did want to go out to eat this evening," Evelyn repeated.

"You can go!" the doctor exclaimed. "That's the neat part about the Save Your Life Cholesterol Plan. You can use it at the nicest of restaurants or at a fast-food chain, at a formal banquet or at a snack supper at home. You will develop a life-style that will let you eat in any situation you find yourself."

"But what you're saying," Andy stated, "is that we need to start right now rather than in the morning."

"*Right now,* if that's your commitment," the doctor said. "Let me give you an example of why I think the essence of diet goal-setting is based on what I do today rather than what I plan to do tomorrow.

"When I went to college, I made it my major goal to be accepted into medical school. For the intermediate goals, I saw the need to excel in each subject as being essential in reaching my major goal."

"So, each biology course you took became an intermediate goal," Andy interrupted, "with boulders in your path?"

"Many boulders." Dr. Franklin agreed with a smile. "Boulders such as dates, friends wanting me to play tennis, fraternity happenings, anything that deterred my studying became a boulder in the path of my intermediate goals."

"How did you handle them?" Evelyn asked.

"Through immediate action goals. That first night of school, I was in my room studying chemistry. At ten o'clock, a group of friends came by to get me to go out for a hamburger. Many of them were premed, a few in my same chemistry class. If they could do it, why shouldn't I take the time off also? Right then, I made a decision that I look back on as one of the most important decisions I've ever made.

"I realized that if I were going to achieve my major goal of being accepted to medical school, I needed a good grade in the chemistry course I was taking. And if I were going to make a good grade in this chemistry course, I needed to study hard every night. And if *right now,* I didn't decide to study when a little boulder was thrown my way, I probably wouldn't study the next time, especially if a bigger boulder—like a midweek date with that cute freshman I had met earlier—was thrown at me. No, I realized that my entire goal structure was based on what I did *right now.* I decided that *right now,* it was more important for me to study. *Right now,* I visualized that acceptance letter from medical school. Simply put, *right now* I wanted that acceptance letter more than I wanted the hamburger."

"So you stayed home and studied?" Evelyn looked at the doctor.

"I stayed and studied," he replied. "Of the four classmen who were premed in my fraternity, I was the only one to be accepted to medical school. I didn't gauge what I did by what they did; I gauged what I did by my major goal, just me and the goal; nothing else entered in."

"What you're saying is that we have to commit to our major goal, keep it always before us, not depend on circumstances or other people—just each of us and the goal?" Andy verified.

"And every day is a *right now* day," the doctor emphasized.

"I like that," Evelyn stated. "I understand now why your plan works. I really believe for the first time in my life I am going to make it. I simply need to develop the incentives that are important to me and go from there. Thank you so much for going over this approach to life-style eating."

"Remember what it says in Proverbs," Dr. Franklin reminded them. "'As he thinks in his heart, so is he.' You have to first lose the weight in your mind, then lose it for real."

The Wilsons left the office, full of confidence that for the first time in their trail of dieting, they had found the secret to success they had been looking for. If it worked to get Dr. Franklin into medical school, surely it would work to develop the healthy bodies they wanted to grow old with. They wanted to feel better, to look their best, and to avoid an early grave. They were determined. Today had been a jubilee day in their lives.

They didn't know it, but the session they had just completed would have a profound impact on their future personalities. It was going to change the way they thought about themselves and about each other. It would change the way others thought of them. Not only would the people who saw them every day admire their willpower, but when they met someone they had never met before, they would make a different first appearance. Even more important, they would have a different inner self. They would walk differently, have greater self-esteem, and change in so many ways they couldn't imagine that day. But they were happy enough knowing that right then they had become a success at losing weight.

They could hardly wait to visit the next physician and learn the next step as they began traveling the most exciting and significant trip of their lives.

2

A CLOSE LOOK AT YOUR EATING HABITS

The Wilsons entered the office of Dr. Benjamin Thomas, a young doctor who had blocked off time to see them to discuss their next step in the new Save Your Life Cholesterol Plan.

"Good morning," Dr. Thomas greeted the couple. "I'm to go over the concept of our life-style cholesterol diet with you."

"I'm sure it works," Andy began. "I'm all prepared mentally for it, after our visit to Dr. Franklin."

"It will work. Guaranteed!" responded Dr. Thomas. "You follow the plan—it works for you."

"Is it as simple as I've heard it is?" asked Evelyn.

"Fairly simple," Dr. Thomas replied. "You've already accomplished the most important part of the plan before you were referred to me. If you got this far, you must already realize can't diet for you. It's something you must do for yourself."

"You mean the commitment and the goals and the persistence to overcome the days when I fail at my diet?" Evelyn asked.

"We don't like to use the term *fail*." Dr. Thomas smiled at her and her husband. "Failing at something is the final outcome of permanently giving up. You will have temporary setbacks, but they will be just that—temporary."

"You know," Andy responded, "for the first time in my life, I feel confident I can lose this extra weight of mine. I really and truly believe that."

"As I said," Dr. Thomas spoke again, "if you didn't have that solidified in your mind, you would not have been sent to me for further instructions.

■ *A skyscraper is built one brick at a time. Excess weight is lost one ounce at a time. The foundation of both is the decision to begin.*

"I want to paint you a mental picture of this type of dieting. If a person loses just two ounces a day, in a year's time, he will lose forty-five pounds. That's a lot of weight. But if you look at it as eliminating a slice of bread a day, or eliminating mayonnaise from your sandwiches, or not ordering those french fries, or not eating those last three bites on your child's plate, then it's easily attainable. Simple, attainable, and easy to do once you realize what you're about and set your goals properly. Losing two ounces a day may mean only running or walking a mile after dinner. Believe you can accomplish your objective because you can. We had one patient who lost thirty-seven pounds by losing 1.9 ounces a day.

"This plan is different from all other diet plans you have read about. It isn't one person's secret way he or she lost fifty pounds and then made up some unusual physiological reason for the loss. This is not a plan that tells how one person lost weight or how any number of people lost weight. The Save Your Life Cholesterol Plan was devised by doctors who approached the problem of excess weight in a scientific way. It based on the physiological response of the body to food and exercise." Dr. Thomas began to explain the backbone of the plan to the couple.

Andy interrupted, "Do you mean that everything you're going to tell us is medically sound, the real way the body reacts?"

"Yes," Dr. Thomas responded. "Of course, it's put into layman's terms, but I can assure you everything we tell you will be medically sound and based on reports found in the medical literature. The Save Your Life Cholesterol Plan is the compilation of these medical reports, and it's presented in such a way that you can see the need to follow the plan."

"And what about actually losing the weight? This isn't based on just one person who's had success with this diet and now wants to convince everyone else it can work for them too, is it?" Evelyn asked.

"Not at all," Dr. Thomas said assuredly. "This plan was born because one doctor in our group began to notice a very select group of people who had actually lost weight and kept it off."

"I bet that *was* a very select group," Andy commented. "Of all the people I know who have been on a diet, only a handful have actually made it, and less than half of those have kept it off."

"Those are the very people we went to see to find their secret to successful weight loss," Dr. Thomas continued. "Those were the people we wanted to track in dieting. Those were the real leaders we wanted to interview, to probe their minds and see how they made it happen."

"That's good," Andy nodded in agreement. "I like that approach. You interviewed people who had successfully dieted and then came up with this Save Your Life Cholesterol Plan?"

"Exactly, but we didn't just interview the successful ones. We also interviewed people who had lost and then regained their weight."

"To see why they regained?" Evelyn asked.

"Sure. If we knew how they lost in the first place and then found out why they didn't keep the weight off, we could come up with a plan that really worked. Then, we reviewed the medical literature from the leading journals doctors read. The result is something we believe will change the basic eating life-styles in America," the doctor explained further.

"That's why you say this is the scientific approach to the problem of weight loss?" Andy asked.

"As scientific as one can get," Dr. Thomas responded. "It really takes a lot of the guesswork out of the picture. We know how the body functions normally. We know how the body functions with too many calories. We know how the body would function if it received fewer calories.

"The important factor that made the difference between the individuals who lost weight and sustained that goal weight, and the individuals who lost their weight and regained it is found in one important word: HABIT. Those who lost weight and sustained that loss had changed their eating habits drastically. They developed an entirely new eating behavior so that once the weight was off, they continued eating the same way they did to lose the weight in the first place.

"The average American family relies on less than twenty basic menus. Once these basic combinations of foods are changed and habits are formed around eating new foods, the battle is won. Habits become life-style. That's what we want to change: the American life-style of eating.

"Many individuals can lose weight on any number of diets without developing eating habits that will stay with them permanently. They revert to their old eating habits sooner or later, and the weight goes back on.

"We feel this habit concept is so important, we've nicknamed this diet and exercise program the 'Habit Diet.' We know that if we can help you develop the habit of eating according to the Save Your Life Cholesterol Plan, you will have it won. I read somewhere that 87 percent of all our actions are performed through habits. We pull a chair under us before we sit down at the table, open our mouth just before food gets there, chew our food—all out of habit, without having to think about it. That's the goal: you will eat the proper food and in the right amounts without having to think twice."

Andy liked what he heard. "It's a sound plan. I'm ready to start losing weight."

"But what about me?" Evelyn interrupted her husband. "He's always this enthusiastic, wanting to get his weight off. All I want to do is lose a few pounds . . ."

"Fifteen pounds is not a few," her husband reminded her before he turned back to Dr. Thomas. "I just want to lose some weight and then keep it off. Plus, I want to know what type of food to eat. My father had a heart attack when he was sixty, and my doctor told me I have borderline high blood pressure. Can you teach me what type of foods to eat to ensure I won't have high blood pressure and a heart attack?" Andy was very serious in his questioning.

"Very good insight," Dr. Thomas agreed. "Learning what foods are bad for your arteries and your heart is of equal importance to simply losing the weight in the first place.

"Let me give you a few facts that have influenced us in setting up the Save Your Life Cholesterol Plan. Over six million people in the United States have coronary artery disease. Over 500,000 Americans kill themselves prematurely each year because of a heart attack. They don't plan to do it; they simply didn't plan *not* to do it. Death is the only symptom in 18 percent of these heart attacks. Over 80 percent see a doctor: half of these people have suffered a nonfatal heart attack, and the other half have experienced anginal chest pain.

"Our plan helps you lose weight and also helps you plan not to have a heart attack—all by changing your eating habits. That's our goal for both of you.

"That's why it's so important for the individual who is only ten to fifteen pounds overweight to get rid of the excess. That fifteen pounds of extra weight probably represents *what* the individual eats rather than *how much*. Your extra forty pounds is most likely from eating too much cholesterol and fat. Your family history of heart disease makes it imperative that you learn which foods are more prone to cause heart trouble. That's where cholesterol comes in. In your situation it's even more important than losing pounds to learn which foods to eat and which to avoid.

"I can prolong more lives teaching patients how to protect the arteries in their hearts than I ever can by performing surgery on those arteries. That's why I'm so excited by this diet program. It gives you an excellent understanding about what effect cholesterol in your diet has on the arteries in your body. By the time we are through, you'll want to attack your weight problem and cholesterol intake viciously. You won't pussyfoot around. You will have a definite purpose in choosing what you eat."

"I've read a little about cholesterol. What is it?" Evelyn asked.

"It's a type of fat we eat too much of in America. We'll spend an entire session teaching you what you need to know about cholesterol. Right now, let's look more at the general concept of what will be expected of you on this Habit Diet."

"Let's get on with it." Andy joined in the excitement of the discussion. "I'm ready to start losing weight—*right now*."

Dr. Thomas smiled. Their attitudes seemed just right. He felt they were going to lose their weight with very little trouble and rapidly develop their new life-style of eating. In six months they would be completely different people, physically and mentally. He began to instruct them: "The Save Your Life Cholesterol Plan centers on three themes. One is for the overweight individual. We have to burn up more calories than we take in to lose weight. Simple as that. Do you know how that's accomplished?"

"I guess just eating less food," replied Evelyn.

"Eating less calories," the doctor agreed partially. "Less calories but you may actually eat more food. Some foods contain less than one-half the calories of other foods even though the amounts are equal. Fats contain 9 calories per gram while proteins and carbohydrates contain only 4. We'll teach you which foods to fill up on and which to eat sparingly. So don't look at it as eating less food, but look at it as eating less calories."

"Never thought of it that way," Andy stated.

"Can you think of any other way than eating less food to end up with fewer net calories in the body at the end of the day?" asked Dr. Thomas.

"Well, I know most diets recommend some sort of exercise to burn more calories," Andy said, "but I haven't exercised much since college days. I'm not athletic at all now. I do stay busy, however. I move around a lot. I don't do much sitting."

"You're on the right road," Dr. Thomas agreed. "There are two basic ways to end up with fewer calories in the body at the end of the day. One is to put fewer in by eating less food, and the other is to burn off more calories through exercise, over and above your regular activity."

"What if I just diet?" Andy continued. "I don't think I can do the exercise routine anymore."

"Not unless you commit to it and include it in your goal structure," the doctor argued.

"Is it really that important?" Evelyn asked.

"Sure is," Dr. Thomas responded. "We think exercise is so vital to the program, you will have one entire session devoted to exercise. With only thirty minutes per day of the proper exercise, you'll lose over 300 calories. That can be the difference in losing and not losing when you have taken in 1200 calories that day. Exercise is vital to the overall diet program. However, there are numerous exercises you can choose from so you won't waste time. We'll even give you some options for doing other things while you're exercising."

"Good," Andy chimed in. "I don't think I could ever find

time in my busy day to devote a specified time just to exercise. I'm busier than most."

"Yes, I know," Dr. Thomas laughed. "I've heard that from every patient we've had.

"Okay," he continued, "fewer calories in, and exercise to utilize more calories. I said the Save Your Life Cholesterol Plan centered on three themes, and the first deals with calories; the second deals with weight stabilization."

"What's that?" Evelyn inquired.

"Weight stabilization enters the picture after you've lost your excess weight, whether forty pounds or fifteen pounds—and reached your desired weight," Dr. Thomas said. "This part of the plan guarantees that your weight will stay at that level. We can honestly guarantee your excess weight will stay off. It's an ongoing process. This is where life-style comes into play—the habit part of the diet. By the time you reach this point, your eating style will be set for life. You will maintain your desired weight and looks long after you take the excess weight off."

"That's even more exciting!" Evelyn exclaimed. "Lots of my friends have lost weight but just gradually put it back on in less than a year."

"The problem was," Dr. Thomas said, "they didn't develop the proper eating habits to permanently change their life-style of eating. Weight stabilization, by changing your eating life-style, is the key to our ability to guarantee permanent weight control with this plan. Our life-style plan develops eating habits that will remain with you forever. Once a habit is formed, it is very difficult to break. Once you develop the habit of drinking 1 percent milk, you'll never think twice about pouring whole milk on your cereal. That won't be a daily decision anymore. Once you develop the habit of not eating eggs for breakfast, you won't have to decide each morning whether you'll have eggs or not. As a matter of fact, you'll probably catch yourself picking boiled egg yolks out of the salad served at a restaurant. You'll stick with your good eating habits because we're going to teach you why you should eat certain foods and avoid others. The knowledge you obtain will be a tremendous reinforcement for your new Save Your Life Cholesterol Plan eating habits."

"Sounds great. I understand calories and I understand habits. What's the third theme?" Andy was almost impatient to get on with all the facts he needed to get his weight off and be fit.

"The third theme teaches you what types of food to eat." Dr. Thomas sat down to discuss this last portion of the diet. "There are some foods we Americans simply eat too much of. We study reports in many medical journals of the different eating styles around the world and find that the people in Africa do not have such diseases as colon cancer, appendicitis, or diverticulitis. We read reports from areas where people do not have heart attacks, strokes, or high blood pressure. We learn from these diets around the world and then pass that important knowledge on to you. We give you medically sound reasons to cut down on certain foods as well as medical explanations of what these foods actually do to your arteries once inside your bloodstream."

"I'm not a doctor, not even a nurse," Evelyn said. "Will I be able to understand all this medical jargon? Will I know why this part of your plan is so important?"

"Sure. You'll be able to understand it perfectly," Dr. Thomas assured both of them. "This program is not built around a lot of promotion. There are no advertisements showing a Barbie-Doll female, no supplemental vitamins or pills to take—just straightforward facts about dieting. We believe your knowledge of the physiological reaction of the body to the foods you eat is part of convincing your mind that you shouldn't eat an abundance of certain foods. If you completely understand the physiology of the body, how it reacts to certain foods, you will find it much easier to avoid them. You will catch yourself wondering how in the world that person at the next table could possibly eat what he is eating."

"Sounds solid to me," Andy remarked.

"Let's get started," Evelyn agreed. "Where do we go first?"

■ *Education: your best weapon against your worst enemy—high blood cholesterol.*

Dr. Thomas closed his notebook. "You're now ready to meet Dr. James Clement. You'll like him, and you'll like what he has to say. You're getting ready to learn more about your body's response to food than you ever imagined. You'll never eat the same again after meeting Dr. Clement. Take good notes on what he says; he covers a lot of territory, and you will want to review what he has to tell you. Study what he has to say until you have full retention of his information. A lot of the remaining program is based on what you learn from him."

The couple left Dr. Thomas's office. His presentation had been short and to the point. All he wanted to do was to get them thinking about the basics they were about to learn. He wanted them to understand that the Save Your Life Cholesterol Plan was much more than cutting down on the amount of food they eat. He wanted them to start thinking physiologically about what the body does once foods are ingested. He wanted them to have some conception of the arteries in their hearts and to begin to see in their mind's eye what those arteries looked like once cholesterol began to be deposited on their walls. The couple needed to know that exercise was going to play an important role in the plan.

And he wanted them to realize they were not in some temporary diet program where they would lose weight and then go their way. No, they needed to understand that they were in a life-changing program that would affect them the rest of their lives. This next session will probably have more positive action on their physical well-being than anything they have ever heard. They see that their next visit is to a cardiologist.

3

CORONARY ARTERY DISEASE: THE DEATH OF AMERICA

As the Wilsons entered the office of Dr. James Clement, they were greeted by a pleasant secretary who handed them some written material about the Save Your Life Cholesterol Plan. The pamphlet explained the two primary purposes of the diet: one is to lose weight and the other is to learn what food will enhance longevity. They also read what foods prevent the number one killer disease in America: coronary heart disease.

The couple was ushered into the office of Dr. Clement, a cardiologist who continually studies the effects of diet on coronary heart disease. They had heard and read a lot about people requiring heart bypass surgery. Even though they knew about heart attacks, they had never really understood exactly what doctors meant when they spoke on coronary heart disease.

"Before we get into the specifics of how to lose weight," Dr. Clement began, "you will have two sessions on one of the most important aspects of the Save Your Life Cholesterol Plan. We want you to have a strong desire to get your body into top physical condition. We want you to be your best. You can't isolate your weight excess into a separate compartment of your life. Excess weight affects your whole being. We want you to know and understand how to reach your overall full potential in life. We base our entire program on education, educating you about the most important reason to follow the Save Your Life Cholesterol Plan. We want you to know the physiology of your body well enough so that when you eat the wrong food, your mind will be able to see that food enter your bloodstream and then see what it does to your body. When we finish, you will have a naturally strong resistance to eating certain food.

"I encourage you to pay special attention to these next two sessions. They can change your life. They can extend your life. It is that important. I want to explain about the most important organ you have in your body and go over the disease that affects it most."

Dr. Clement had barely greeted the couple before he started into what he had to say about the Save Your Life Cholesterol Plan. He was the most intense of all the doctors in the program. He knew he had so much to teach them in such a short time.

He continued his remarks as the Wilsons listened with concentrated attention. "Coronary heart disease is the disease that causes heart attacks, as the layman knows them. If you looked up the word *coronary* in the dictionary," he picked up an index card with the definition typed out, "you would find it 'denotes the arteries that supply the heart muscles and, by extension, the pathologic involvement of them.' If we are to talk about coronary heart disease, we must understand the cause of that disease. We must realize that heart muscles require oxygen for the muscles to continue to function. That oxygen is carried in the blood through the arteries in the heart. If those arteries are blocked, the blood cannot move the oxygen to the heart muscles, and that portion of the heart quits pumping. The heart muscle lets us know it isn't receiving enough oxygen by causing pain in the chest. I want you to think of the arteries in the heart whenever you think of heart attacks."

"So coronary heart disease really means disease of the arteries of the heart," Andy acknowledged.

"Right," Dr. Clement responded. "And that is what we're going to talk about—how diet affects the arteries of the heart as well as all other arteries in the body."

Evelyn interrupted, "Does coronary artery disease have anything to do with losing weight? That's what I'm interested in; losing weight and getting trim."

"Our discussion on coronary heart disease is not going to center on actually losing weight so much as what we should eat and not eat in order to be healthier, feel better and, most important of all, live longer." Dr. Clement emphasized this part of the Save Your Life diet program.

"What most people don't realize is that the most important part of dieting is to protect those arteries of the heart. Sure, this part of the program doesn't take two pounds off you this week and make you able to tighten your belt one more notch, but it will benefit you long after you have lost your weight and bought new clothes to fit your slimmer body. This aspect of the program will enable you to enjoy that good body in a much more active way and for a longer time. I want you to learn in detail the important information we give you." Dr. Clement's manner was friendly even though his words were direct.

"Where did you get the information you're about to tell us?" Andy wanted to know. "I've read articles and books that explain all sorts of physiology of the body and dieting and my doctor just laughs at a lot of them. I read in one book that your body could only digest one type of food at a time and that we shouldn't eat fruits just after a meal. I don't want to waste time trying to learn something that is not actually sound. I want to know the facts, and I want you as a doctor to give them to me straight."

"I'm glad you feel that way," responded Dr. Clement. "You're absolutely right; there are many misconceptions about dieting and how the body reacts to the foods we eat, but I'll make you a promise. Everything I tell you will be substantiated in the medical literature that can be found in any teaching hospital's library in the country and in almost any hospital library from the biggest hospital to the small community hospital." Dr. Clement seemed thrilled to have a couple who was interested in the accurate medical aspects of dieting, and he tried to assure them that he would put his medical terms in words they could understand.

"The material I will be giving you comes from such medical publications as the *Journal of the American Medical Association*, the *American Journal of Cardiology*, the *New England Journal of Medicine*, the *American Journal of Medicine*, the *American Heart Journal*." Dr. Clement mentioned the names of a few of the journals he had researched to document what he was going to say. "The material I will give you describes the medical aspect of what certain foods will do to your body. I am going to center on the most important element we have to watch and that is a fat called cholesterol. When you leave here, I want you to know without a doubt in your mind how important it is to understand about eating fats in general, and cholesterol in particular."

"Okay, I'm ready to learn." Evelyn got out her notepad. Up to this point in her life, her weight had made her emotionally unsettled. She was ready to do something about her weight and all that went with being overweight.

"Me, too. You've convinced me," Andy chimed in.

"Good." Dr. Clement sat down at his desk and pulled a stack of notes from his drawer.

"First of all, I don't want you to look at this program as a diet. A diet connotes a temporary event in most individuals' minds. Our program is not a diet in that sense. It is an eating life-style in which you change your eating habits. In this way, not only will you lose weight, but once you've lost it, you'll continue eating properly and keep that weight off. If you must call it a diet, then look at it as a permanent diet because you will stay on it the rest of your life. Now, let's see where coronary heart disease fits into this overall plan. Do you know the leading cause of death in people over sixty-five?" He looked up at Andy.

"Cancer, I suppose," he responded.

"Coronary heart disease. The plugging of the arteries of the heart kills more people than anything else."

"Does that include women, too?" Evelyn wanted to know. "I thought breast cancer or ovarian cancer killed more women than anything else."

"You're on the right track when you compare women with men in talking about heart attacks. Before a woman goes through menopause, she does have an apparent protection against heart attacks so the onset of this problem occurs later in women than men. However, the leading cause of death in women is coronary heart disease, and the amount of cholesterol in the blood is a risk factor that both men and women have to deal with."

Dr. Clement had laid the important groundwork for the couple to realize they were talking about life and death in this discussion. The Save Your Life Cholesterol Plan is more than simply a way to look better with less fat on the body. It goes hand in hand with dieting, but it stresses the one most important factor that is left out of most diet instructions—what cholesterol in the blood can do to the arteries. Dr. Clement wanted them to realize that what they were discussing would probably be the eventual cause of the death of both of them.

"First, let me tell you some general facts about the arteries in our bodies and how cholesterol relates to them. There is a chronology of events in the cholesterol syndrome. We know what happens when a person eats cholesterol over the years; it has a fatal outcome. Approximately thirty million people in the United States suffer from blocked arteries. Close to one million of these people die from this problem every year. About two-thirds of these deaths are due to the blockage of the arteries of the heart. Many of the other deaths are due to the same type of blockage in arteries throughout the body, resulting in strokes and high blood pressure.

"I want you to realize that when you eat certain foods, you are not only adding on pounds but also depositing parts of this food in the walls of your arteries throughout your body, and that can result in death. You may find it difficult to associate what you eat with death, but I want you to at least associate what you eat with how debilitating it can be to you, how it leads to poor health for the rest of your life.

"There are people walking around today who are able to live only half-lives. They are in very poor shape; they are out of breath just from walking up a flight of stairs. Their waistbands are always a little too tight. Their knit shirts are too snug around the middle. They don't look or feel 100 percent and never again will. They never know what their full potential in life is because their physical condition is too poor to let them reach it. Americans, as a group of people, cannot perform their best, cannot benefit from all life has to offer, simply because of their diet. Dr. Dennis Burkitt, who researched Burkitt's lymphoma, tells us that one-third of all diseases in America are caused by what we eat or what we do not eat. Americans do not eat properly for good health. We have to learn what the average American diet is doing to us and then begin to change our eating habits as well as our exercise habits if we are ever to be the healthiest people possible.

"I want you to become familiar with coronary artery disease because it relates so closely to your overall physical condition and awareness of it is the cornerstone of the Save Your Life Cholesterol Plan. If you understand coronary artery disease, you will know enough about your body to develop your successful eating habits. You will know why we want you to lose weight and keep it off.

"There are three main risk factors a person has to deal with in looking at coronary heart disease, and all three are important to your good health. The first—neither of you has to worry about this one—is cigarette smoking."

"Never have smoked," interrupted Andy.

"That's good," Dr. Clement stressed. "That's one factor of the three you won't have to worry about, but if you did smoke, I would be telling you about the increased risk you have for a heart attack."

"What are the other two risk factors that do deal with us?" Evelyn asked.

"Blood-cholesterol and blood pressure," responded Dr. Clement.

"Most people know their blood pressure, can even get it checked in the grocery store if they want; but very few know what their cholesterol level is."

"That's right," answered Andy. "Every time I go into my doctor's office, the nurse grabs my arm and takes my blood pressure. The doctor then tells me it's normal. I always feel good about that."

"But all people ought to know their cholesterol level just as you know your blood pressure," Dr. Clement pointed out. "The next time you go to your doctor, ask him to draw some blood and check your cholesterol level as well as your high-density lipoprotein-cholesterol level. Your cholesterol level is just as important for you to know as your blood pressure. If it is elevated, you can do something to correct that problem by controlling what you eat."

"What is blood-cholesterol anyway?" Evelyn asked.

"Cholesterol is a special type of fat or lipid that the body manufactures naturally, and we also consume it in our diet. It is carried in the blood wrapped in a protein sack. This combination of cholesterol and protein is called lipoprotein-cholesterol. It is found in two basic forms in the blood: low-density lipoprotein-cholesterol, tied to heart disease; and high-density lipoprotein-cholesterol, thought to protect against it."

"So what's the importance of these two lipoprotein-cholesterol combinations?" asked Evelyn.

"We're going to call the low-density lipoprotein-cholesterol combination the *bad* cholesterol," the doctor instructed.

"And the high-density lipoprotein-cholesterol combination is the *good* cholesterol?" Andy smiled at the doctor's "good guys-bad guys" approach.

"Exactly. Let's call them LDL-C and HDL-C so we can designate the two quickly while I explain them to you." The doctor motioned the couple over to his desk where he wrote LDL-C on a tablet.

■ *Sorry, good for nothing Low Down Living-cholesterol is bad for your arteries.*

He began, "LDL-C represents the low-density lipoprotein-cholesterol that contains the greatest percentage of cholesterol in the blood and is probably responsible for depositing cholesterol in the walls of the arteries. Because it makes these deposits that eventually clog the arteries, we look at it as being bad."

"That makes sense," Evelyn agreed.

"We want to avoid these in our diet as much as possible," Dr. Clement continued.

"Why don't we avoid them completely if they're so bad for us?" Andy had asked a very pertinent question.

"Some people do just that; they become vegetarians. Cholesterol is found in all foods of animal origin and is part of every animal cell. Your body uses cholesterol to make all kinds of essential substances such as hormones and cell walls. Some cholesterol is essential to body health, but if you didn't ever take a bite of cholesterol in your diet, your liver would manufacture enough to meet your body requirements." Dr. Clement answered his question carefully. "So, most of us eat cholesterol; we just must keep in mind what it does to our arteries and make sure we don't eat so much that it damages these vessels. Remember, the higher the level of cholesterol in the blood, the greater the risk of plugging your arteries, and consequently, the greater the chance of a heart attack."

"So, what can I do to lower my cholesterol?" Evelyn wanted to know.

"Well, first, you should have your cholesterol checked. I want to stress that every American ought to have cholesterol levels checked. Routine cholesterol screening measures only total cholesterol: LDL-C plus HDL-C. I want you to have them both measured. If only the total cholesterol is measured, some people are going to have heart attacks because their good HDL-C is too low in proportion to their total cholesterol. About 50 percent of men who have heart attacks have total cholesterol below 225, and 15 percent of all heart attacks occur in people whose total cholesterol level is below 200. The only way to know if these people are at risk is to measure their HDL to see if they have enough protective cholesterol in relation to their total cholesterol. That is where the Save Your Life Cholesterol Plan differs from most plans. Most recommend a screen test of total cholesterol. We want individuals following our plan to have their HDL-C determined also.

"Basically, you want to know two numbers: your total cholesterol and your high-density lipoprotein-cholesterol. That will tell you how much of the bad LDL-C you have and how much of the good, protective HDL-C you have. Most of the total cholesterol number represents the bad LDL-C. By subtracting the good HDL-C from the total cholesterol, you get an idea of how much LDL-C you have. The ratio of these two cholesterols determines your risk for developing coronary heart disease.

"The ratio of HDL-C to total cholesterol is a very good prediction of heart disease. The more HDL-C you have to protect your arteries, in relation to the LDL-C, the better. The closer you come to a 1 to 1 ratio, the better. It would be great to have a high HDL-C and a low LDL-C. Basically, you are at a low risk if your ratio is below 4.5."

"Give us an example," Andy said.

"Well, if your total cholesterol is 200 and your HDL-C is 50, your ratio of HDL-C to total cholesterol would be 200/50 with a resulting ratio of 4.0.

"Since 70 to 80 percent of your total cholesterol is LDL-C, you want to lower your total cholesterol number. In actuality, you want to lower the LDL-C portion and raise the HDL-C portion."

"So you want your total cholesterol to be as low as possible?" Andy asked the doctor.

"Exactly. The cholesterol in the blood of the average American is way too high. The ideal number keeps dropping. Many studies encourage us to shoot for less than 200, but I saw a recent study that stated we should strive for a cholesterol level of 150." Dr. Clement had begun to suggest cholesterol goals in his use of healthy levels.

"So what do we shoot for?" Evelyn was eager for the personal application.

"In the Save Your Life Cholesterol Plan, we don't shoot for anything. We simply become aware of what foods have cholesterol and try to avoid them as much as possible. Some individuals on this diet become fanatic and memorize complete lists of foods to avoid. You couldn't get them to eat an egg or put a pat of butter on their potato for the world. Other people know which foods to avoid and avoid them in moderation. The problem with saying that 200 is the number to aim for is that I see too many people with a cholesterol level of 200 who feel perfectly comfortable eating foods high in cholesterol because they feel safe with that number. In this program, we want you not to feel safe eating cholesterol. We want you to develop an awareness of what is going on in your body as a result of the foods you eat. Therefore, we don't recommend a certain level. Your goal is to learn which foods contain cholesterol and to stay away from them as much as an individual possibly can."

"Do you have a list of such foods?" Andy asked. "Tell me what foods to avoid, and I'll handle the rest."

"Let's look at cholesterol in milligrams, just for the sake of comparison." Dr. Clement began to write a list of foods on the tablet for the couple to see. "We'll go from highest in cholesterol to lowest."

FOOD	CHOLESTEROL (milligrams)
One egg yolk	270
Shrimp, 3½ oz	150
Beef, lean, 3 oz	75
Chicken/turkey, light meat without skin, 3 oz	65
Fish, lean, 3 oz	55
Oysters, 3 oz	40
Fruits, grains, vegetables	0

"I thought beef was worse than that for you," Andy stated.

"Beef has saturated fats also, which play a similar role to that of cholesterol, but we'll cover that later. Note that this list shows lean beef. Most of what you order in a restaurant isn't lean. This list will get you started thinking about cholesterol."

"So, is that all there is to it?" Andy liked the idea of conquering something in less than two minutes.

"Not exactly," Dr. Clement warned. "It takes a little more than just learning a short list, but that's a start. Just remember that cholesterol is found in all foods of animal origin and is part of every animal cell. If you are eating meat, you are eating cholesterol. Plus, more and more companies are listing the amount of cholesterol in the food they package. I want you to develop a working knowledge about cholesterol content in foods to the point that you become uneasy when you start to take a bite of high-cholesterol food."

"Before we go further, tell me why you started teaching the Save Your Life Cholesterol Plan," Andy inquired. "Were you overweight and wanted to tell how you lost it, or are you involved because of the money you make teaching, or do you just enjoy telling us about what you know best?"

"Let me assure you my motive is certainly more medical than financial. All of us in the Save Your Life Cholesterol Plan are concerned about changing the health status of the average American. We want to open your eyes to the dangers of what you eat. We want the Save Your Life Cholesterol Plan to be the warning label on cholesterol foods similar to the Surgeon General's warning label on a cigarette package."

"What were some of the changes you had to make in your diet when you first started avoiding cholesterol?" Evelyn asked Dr. Clement for a little personal testimony about changes in his eating style.

The doctor thought a minute. "I guess the biggest changes involved only three or four foods. First, I just quit eating any butter that I knew of."

"You mean like putting butter on your rolls at a restaurant?" Andy asked.

"Right. I used to eat two or three rolls in a restaurant before the main meal arrived. I would cake on the butter to make the roll taste better. Now, I avoid the bread as well as the butter before my meal because I realize I'm going to eat my main meal whether I add that bread to it or not. So, I cut out the calories of the rolls plus the cholesterol found in the butter."

"Okay," Andy said, "you've convinced me about the butter. What other changes did you make?"

"What I eat may be completely different from what you eat, so don't just follow my lead but develop your own list of changes." Dr. Clement wanted the couple to know that the lifestyle diet is very individualistic. Each person on this diet has to evaluate his or her style of eating and find the specifics that have to change.

"Nevertheless, I'll go ahead and point out some of the changes I've had to make myself," Dr. Clement continued. "I almost never eat eggs anymore. If they're in a salad or cut up in some dish, I won't pick over them, but I don't eat the regular bacon-and-eggs breakfast I used to. Nor do I order an omelette packed with cheese and green peppers for a snack at 10:00 P.M. as I did at one time in my life. I've read it's okay to eat two eggs a week. The way I figure it, there are so many eggs hidden in foods we eat, I just eliminate all known eggs in my diet. I eat almost no cheese. I never order cheese on a sandwich anymore, and that used to be a favorite of mine. Cheese is another food Americans eat lots of that is high in cholesterol. I quit ice cream and started using low-fat milk.

■ *Forty percent of the cholesterol that Americans eat is from eggs. At least one-third of that is hidden in food we never consider as a source of eggs.*

"You'll find you will simply quit eating some foods once you realize their fat content and how much cholesterol they contain. The main idea is to become so conscious of fat and cholesterol that the desire not to eat those particular foods becomes second nature to you. Once you really can visualize what you are putting in your mouth is doing to your arteries, not only will your desire for those foods decrease, but for some reason, you will actually develop a dislike for them. I want you to think of all the foods I've been mentioning as containing the *bad* LDL-cholesterol."

"You've covered the LDL-cholesterol well," Evelyn said, "but what about the good cholesterol, the HDL-cholesterol? You said we wanted this cholesterol elevated in our bodies. Why is that?"

"HDL-cholesterol seems to play a key role in the protective dynamics of cholesterol metabolism," Dr. Clement began. "We suspect that one of its normal functions is to remove cholesterol from arterial walls. It is not certain how HDL-C protects the arterial wall from the buildup of cholesterol deposits, but one real possibility is that it can actually transport deposited cholesterol out of the wall and to the liver where it is excreted from the body through the bile. I tend to think of HDL-cholesterol being like a scavenger that goes around removing unwanted deposited LDL-cholesterol.

"We also know that we want a lower LDL-cholesterol and a higher HDL-cholesterol. Remember, we want the ratio of the two to be the lowest possible number. As noted earlier, we need a ratio number below 4.5. Also remember that most screening clinics give only total cholesterol levels. We want you to know both total cholesterol and HDL-C. You need to know your total cholesterol number because most of that is made up of artery-clogging LDL-C. You also need to know your HDL-C, which is thought to protect your arteries from the LDL-C. One way to look at it is the greater the number of molecules of HDL-C you have to combat the LDL-C, the better. Likewise, the less number of molecules of LDL-C you have to combat, the better.

"Now, the best part of the plan enters the picture here. We stress the importance of exercise in losing weight. Not only do you burn up calories when you exercise, you also feel much better. All in all, you have a much healthier outlook when you exercise regularly."

"Are you saying exercise has something to do with this HDL-C you're talking about?" Andy asked.

"Yes, more and more reports in the medical literature point to the fact that exercise can in fact increase your HDL-cholesterol, and they even suggest that the more exercise you do each week, the more effect it will have on your HDL-cholesterol." Dr. Clement wanted to plant the seed of desire for exercise with the couple.

"But how much exercise does it take to raise your HDL-cholesterol?" Evelyn asked.

"That hasn't been determined exactly," responded Dr. Clement. "There are many different components that fit into the picture. The type of exercise, the intensity and duration of the particular exercise, plus the frequency of the exercise all fit into this factor."

"I've started jogging a couple of times a week since I started this program." Andy was getting specific. "Actually, I mix walking and jogging for about thirty minutes at a time. Is that enough for me?"

"Possibly," said Dr. Clement. "You'll get into exercise and its relationship to HDL-cholesterol in another session. For now, I want you to think of exercise and HDL-cholesterol as going hand in hand and being somewhat proportional. Whatever amount you exercise will be beneficial, whether it's enough to raise your HDL-cholesterol significantly or simply to burn up extra calories."

Evelyn had begun to plan a visit to her doctor to have her blood drawn to check the levels of cholesterol. "You mentioned earlier that a desirable cholesterol level should be below the 200 mark and that some were even advocating the range around 150. You've mentioned total cholesterol, HDL-cholesterol, and LDL-cholesterol. Explain a little more about where these fit when your doctor says you have a cholesterol reading of 200."

"Yes, I need to cover that in more detail for you. First, you must understand that the number your doctor gives you represents the total amount of all kinds of cholesterol in your blood; basically, it's the total amount of cholesterol in HDL-C, LDL-C, and VLDL."

"Just a minute. You haven't mentioned VLDL before. What's that?" Andy had thought he almost had it clear, but Dr. Clement was throwing something new at him.

"VLDL stands for very low-density lipoproteins. Cholesterol

is carried through the blood in different ways. VLDL particles carry some cholesterol, but mainly they carry triglycerides, another fat different from cholesterol. These very low-density lipoproteins may be broken down into smaller particles, and these particles are called low-density lipoproteins—LDL. These particles carry mainly cholesterol. Even smaller particles carry some cholesterol, and these small, dense protein-cholesterol particles are your high-density lipoprotein-cholesterol combination.

"When your doctor orders your cholesterol count, the numbers he gets back show the total amount of cholesterol in HDL-C, LDL-C, and VLDL. You need to remember that most of your cholesterol is carried by LDL-C, and this is the type found in patients with increased risk of coronary heart disease. The total cholesterol count your doctor gives you also measures the HDL-C combination. And this particle is associated with a decreased risk of coronary heart disease.

"That total cholesterol number also includes the amount of cholesterol in the VLDL configuration, but we do not treat this as a significant amount of cholesterol when talking about coronary heart disease.

"Just remember that most of the cholesterol in total cholesterol is made up of the arteriosclerotic-forming LDL-C. That is why you want your total cholesterol as low as possible."

"So the lower the number, the better," Andy concluded.

"Correct," Dr. Clement responded. "But you also need to ask your doctor to break down that total cholesterol number and tell you what part of the total cholesterol is actually HDL-cholesterol. You want to know what portion is the good cholesterol. You want to know what your ratio of good cholesterol is to your total cholesterol."

"Basically, you want to know the ratio of the protective HDL-C to atherosclerotic LDL-C," Andy concluded.

"Correct," Dr. Clement responded. "You are simply using

the total cholesterol number in your ratio figuring because most of that total cholesterol number is actually LDL-C."

"A more accurate ratio," Andy continued with his reasoning, "would be the ratio of HDL-C to LDL-C. That is what you are actually saying, isn't it? The number of milligrams of HDL-C versus the number of milligrams of LDL-C."

"You are absolutely right," Dr. Clement agreed. "It is just easier to measure the total cholesterol than to break out the LDL-C. Therefore, we use total cholesterol in deciding the ratio.

■ *You want to:* Lower your LDL-C
Heighten your HDL-C

"Let me go over some specifics to help clear your mind about the relationship of the different types of cholesterol. Physicians have some new information from a recent report of the National Cholesterol Program Expert Panel on Detection, Evaluation, and Treatment of High Blood Cholesterol in Adults. This panel of national experts in blood-cholesterol control was brought together by the National Heart, Lung, and Blood Institute. Their report was made primarily to physicians, but you can obtain a copy of it by writing the National Institutes of Health in Bethesda, Maryland."

"Just give us the basics." Andy pulled out his pen to take notes again. "And give them to us in language we can understand. I'd like to keep it in terms of *good* and *bad* cholesterol."

"Okay, I'll go the practical route. I'll teach you what's normal, abnormal, important, and unimportant." Dr. Clement hoped to make it as simple as possible.

"First of all, the panel looked at the factors related to total cholesterol and defined what they considered desirable and high levels. Any level less than 200 mg/dl is considered desirable blood-cholesterol by their standard. Mg/dl means milligrams of cholesterol per deciliter of blood, simply a measurement of cholesterol concentration in the blood.

"If you have your blood drawn in a public screening program for cholesterol and the readout is greater than 200, you should have the test repeated by your physician and take the average as your guideline. The screening programs normally give you one readout, and that is your total cholesterol.

"Now let's look at what you know as the *bad* cholesterol factor, LDL-cholesterol. That total cholesterol is broken down to LDL-cholesterol, HDL-cholesterol, and VLDL-cholesterol. We will disregard the VLDL-cholesterol and concentrate on the LDL-cholesterol and the HDL-cholesterol.

"The recommended level of LDL-cholesterol is less than 130 mg/dl, while the borderline high-risk LDL-cholesterol level is 130 to 159 mg/dl, and high-risk LDL-cholesterol is anything greater than 160 mg/dl."

Evelyn interrupted. "Do you mean that in checking total cholesterol and LDL-cholesterol, the desirable levels are less than 200 and less than 130 respectively?"

"That's correct. And what those two numbers are telling you is that of the 200 mg/dl, 130 mg of that is made up of LDL-cholesterol.

"And the borderline high-risk total cholesterol level is between 200 and 239 as compared to the borderline high-risk LDL-cholesterol level of 130 to 159 that I mentioned. In the same way high-risk total cholesterol is anything over 240; high-risk LDL-cholesterol is anything over 160."

Dr. Clement knew this conglomerate of numbers would take a few minutes to be digested. But once understood, they quickly reveal the significance of anyone's cholesterol report.

Andy looked at his notes. "I'm going to remember two numbers for total cholesterol and two for LDL-cholesterol—the low and high cutoffs for each. Total cholesterol is 200 to 240; LDL-cholesterol is 130 to 160." He quickly made a graph on his pad.

	DESIRABLE less than	BORDERLINE HIGH less than	HIGH RISK greater than
Total cholesterol	200	240	240
LDL-cholesterol	130	160	160

"However you learn, I want you to remember the desirable numbers for each," Dr. Clement added. "Just remember the desirable total cholesterol level is *below* 200 and the desirable LDL-cholesterol is *below* 130. I emphasize *below* because we believe you should strive for the 150 to 160 range for your total cholesterol. Practically speaking, there are very few myocardial infarctions among people whose total cholesterol is in the 150 to 160 range.

"Let me repeat, the recommended goals of the panel I'm reviewing for you are minimum goals by their own admission, and they also state that if a readout lower than 200 mg/dl can be achieved, the risk of coronary heart disease may be further reduced. I personally believe that the risk *is* reduced, the lower the total goes. One reason is a study showing that no one in the study whose total cholesterol was below 150 died from a myocardial infarction.

"I don't want you to get hung up on these numbers. On the other hand, I don't want you to think that you are *only* 5 points over normal if your total cholesterol is 205. That type of reasoning shows a certain complacency about your eating habits. Use the cholesterol lab reports as guidelines only; know what your cholesterol is and keep up with it."

"What does that report say about *good* cholesterol, the HDL-cholesterol?" Andy had realized that HDL-cholesterol was all that was left for him to get straight in his mind about these different reports.

"They consider an HDL-cholesterol count *below* 35 mg/dl a definite coronary heart disease risk factor.

"Let's go to another report for a closer look at HDL-cholesterol. HDL-cholesterol has not been studied nearly as extensively as LDL-cholesterol. The numbers on HDL-cholesterol have not been defined as precisely, but from what I can gather from the medical literature, we should strive for an HDL-cholesterol level in the 50 to 60 range.

"Most reports give a good discussion on the treatment of high cholesterol. They emphasize dietary change as the cornerstone of therapy to reduce blood-cholesterol levels. The second line of defense commonly mentioned is drug therapy. The significant role HDL-cholesterol plays in the overall prevention of coronary heart disease has been minimized by most reports concerning treatment.

■ _Death_ is the first symptom in 18 percent of heart attacks. The cholesterol problem is a silent killer.

"We of the Save Your Life Cholesterol Plan feel that the importance of exercise in increasing HDL-cholesterol has been overlooked to some degree. One of our other doctors will cover this in detail, but I want you to begin now thinking of exercise and HDL-cholesterol concurrently. You can raise your HDL-cholesterol with exercise. A small increase in HDL-cholesterol has a significant effect on the overall ratio of LDL-cholesterol to HDL-cholesterol, and this ratio is very important in predicting your risk of developing coronary heart disease."

"Dr. Clement." Andy put his writing pad down and looked up at the doctor. "You're the first man I've heard who puts dieting in the proper perspective. I began looking into dieting simply from the standpoint of losing weight. You have expanded that to include becoming mentally alert, developing a healthy body from a medical standpoint, protecting my heart with the proper food, and exercising for the sake of my cholesterol level. It's almost like taking a course in health and physiology but in a practical manner. We thank you and the other doctors in the

Save Your Life Cholesterol Plan. You are truly helping us change our life-style for the better."

He didn't realize how much better yet, but he would. He knew more already about cholesterol than 95 percent of all Americans. It will be years before the general population understands just what he knew at that point about the diet he should be eating and why such a diet is important.

He also didn't realize completely all the long-range benefits he would enjoy. By maintaining this healthy life-style, he could diminish the adverse effects of arteriosclerosis on the arteries to all parts of his body as he ages. We see these effects in senility, loss of memory, and decreased sexual life, to name a few.

The life expectancy of Americans is increasing every day. The Save Your Life Cholesterol Plan will enable them to live life more fully and to enjoy good health in those later days. They can save their relatives significant amounts of money as well as pain and grief by being able to live out those extra years healthy rather than sickly.

"Before we continue, I want to emphasize something that is a common denominator for all the physicians in the Save Your Life Cholesterol Plan. We all believe your mental attitude plays an important part in your diet. In short, motivation is going to be important. For that reason, I encourage you to take some steps to stay motivated. Read good books; try learning a new word daily; turn your automobile into a tape library, and whenever you are caught in a traffic jam, utilize that time for education and stimulation by listening to motivational tapes. Work on your goals; work on your overall attitudes."

Evelyn relaxed a moment and leaned back in her chair. You're so right. It's been a long time since I even thought about spending time improving myself. I thought I didn't need to continue studying or listening to tapes or reading books since I had graduated from college. I'm going to start investing in myself—time and money."

"Great!" Dr. Clement responded. "Now, let's get on with our session. Anything you would like explained more?"

Andy looked at Dr. Clement. "I'm beginning to have an overall view about what foods I should avoid and what I should be eating. Are there any major factors you haven't covered that we need to understand?"

"Before we finish this session, I want to cover one more subject closely related to cholesterol. Saturated fats play an important role concerning your cholesterol count. I want you both to comprehend the serious effects that saturated fats, as well as cholesterol, have on your arteries."

"I know saturated fats are prevalent in steaks."

Andy has become very knowledgeable about fat metabolism. He has almost grasped the survey of which foods he ought to be eating and which to avoid. He has heard saturated fats mentioned frequently as one of the foods considered bad for your arteries, but he doesn't yet understand the relationship between saturated fats and cholesterol.

"Yes, I would like to know about the relationship between cholesterol and saturated fats and how that relationship ought to affect what we eat." Evelyn has also pulled most of the concepts together.

"I'm glad you're both interested in learning about this missing link between coronary heart disease and hardening of the arteries. You now know the importance of avoiding cholesterol in your diet. But if you look at some foods on the list you should avoid, you will see that they do not contain all that much cholesterol. So what is it in a good T-bone steak that's so bad for you? You saw in our previous chart that there is not that much more cholesterol in a piece of lean beef compared with an equal amount of chicken. Saturated fat is the big risk factor that is more prevalent in the beef than in the chicken.

"Let's look at what happens if you eat too much saturated fat. First of all, these fats increase your cholesterol level. They do this in part by increasing the amount of LDL-cholesterol which you remember is the lipoprotein particle that carries the bad cholesterol. When your diet contains a large amount of saturated fats, the liver produces more LDL-cholesterol. It has repeatedly been shown that saturated fats raise LDL-cholesterol levels, the cholesterol that contributes directly to atherosclerosis and coronary heart disease.

"Let's look once again at the average American diet. We see it contains about 40 percent of total calories as fat, of which 15 to 17 percent is from saturated fats. It has been shown that if we reduce the saturated fats we eat from 17 percent to 10 percent of total calories, our plasma cholesterol will fall about twenty points. If you can remember that for each percent less saturated fat you eat, you will drop your cholesterol by slightly more than one point. You may not remember all these percentages or points; I just want you to understand that there is a significant correlation between the amount of saturated fats we eat and the level of cholesterol in our blood. This emphatically says you should avoid saturated fats. It doesn't mean you can't ever eat another steak in your life, but it does mean you now know what is in that steak and that your steak-eating habits need to change according to your new life-style of eating."

"What are some of the foods with a large amount of saturated fats that we should know about?" Andy asked.

"Keep in mind dairy products and red meat plus three vegetable fats. Think of whole milk and its related products: cream and butter, ice cream, and cheese. Think of bakery goods. Next, think of red meat. And finally think of vegetable fats: coconut oil, palm oil, and the one you hate to hear me say—chocolate. These are free of cholesterol but high in saturated fat.

"Some foods have a large amount of both saturated fat plus cholesterol, and avoiding these should stick out in your mind. These include red meat and cheeses.

"I want you to think of saturated fats as the main source of raising your blood-cholesterol. Set your minds on the importance of avoiding these foods with a high saturated fat content. Get in the habit of drinking low-fat milk, and limit the amount of red meat and cheese you eat. Think of ice cream and chocolate as foods to avoid, and cut out the butter. You both need to put these on your list of foods to avoid. I want you to develop your eating habits around avoiding both cholesterol and saturated fats."

"That's great." Andy looked at Dr. Clement. "I think I now have a good basic understanding of what happens when I eat certain foods. I know what is going on inside the lining of my arteries when I eat cholesterol and saturated fats. From now on, I will think red meat and dairy products when I think saturated fats."

■ *You have a metabolic problem with your weight. Your body retains ice cream.*

"There is one subject, however, I would like to know a little more about." Evelyn got her notebook out again. "Would you explain the difference in the fats I've been reading about? Exactly what is the difference between saturated fats and polyunsaturated fats and monounsaturated fats?"

"Okay, let's look at it from a caloric standpoint, rather than from weight. The American Heart Association points out that approximately 40 percent of all the calories in an average American diet are from fat. There are 9 calories in each gram of fat, as you recall, compared to 4 calories in each gram of carbohydrate or protein. So, you can see from a mass and weight standpoint, if you ate equal amounts of the three basic food groups, you would receive over twice the amount of calories from the fat as compared to the carbohydrate or protein.

"Now, if 40 percent of your calories come from the fat in the foods you eat, the easiest way to lose weight would be to cut down on the fatty foods. Do you understand the significance of what I just explained?"

"Sure," responded Evelyn. "If I ate two ounces of fatty food, I would be taking in more than twice the number of calories than if I ate the exact same amount of carbohydrate or protein."

"That's right. Now, let's break that fat down into three components: saturated fats, monounsaturated fats, and polyunsaturated fats. Remember, the American Heart Association states the average American takes in about 40 percent of daily calories from fat. If we break that 40 percent down, we see approximately 15 percent each from saturated fats and monounsaturated fats with about 10 percent being from the polyunsaturated fats we eat. This gives you an idea of what we're talking about when we speak of the different kinds of fat."

"Are there *good* and *bad* fats in this scenario?" Andy wanted to know.

"In one sense, maybe. But I want you to think of reducing all fats simply because of the extra calories found in fat. Think first of calories when you think of fat; then take it one step further and think of its effect on cholesterol. Think of the fat in all the fried foods you eat. Think of 50 percent of the calories in fried foods coming from fat. That's why we'll have you eating broiled fish rather than fried. Also, think of fat in baked goods because almost 50 percent of the calories in bakery items is derived from fat. One of the worst is processed food. In most luncheon meats, fat accounts for approximately 75 percent of the calories."

"You've made your point, doctor. Think fat, think calories," Andy laughed.

"Exactly. Fat represents calories. Avoid fats for that purpose if for no other reason.

"Now, if you have it firmly in your mind to avoid fats, I'll break it down a little for you.

"Let's take saturated fat, which we've just discussed. Such fats remain in solid form at room temperature. We've already said that it tends to increase your cholesterol level. Just remember the next time you eat a steak that over half of the fat in that steak is of the saturated type. Restricting the saturated fat in your diet is important in reducing the cholesterol in your blood. Saturated fats and cholesterol are not the same, but both can increase the cholesterol level in your blood. Animal fats, such as that steak I was mentioning, as well as whole milk, cream, cheese, and eggs, contain both saturated fats and cholesterol.

"One step away from saturated fat is monounsaturated fat. It is thought that these fats neither raise nor lower cholesterol, but some recent studies suggest that these fats may have a lowering effect on cholesterol."

"What are some examples of these fats?" Evelyn continued to make notes.

"Most nuts fall into this category, including peanuts, peanut butter, and peanut oil. Olive oil also fits here and, for that reason we stress it as the best cooking oil to use.

"The last group you asked about is polyunsaturated fat. It has been shown to help reduce cholesterol, but it still adds those 9 calories per gram rather than the 4 calories from protein and carbohydrate. In light of that, I wouldn't look at this group as much of a plus.

"Think of polyunsaturated fats as being vegetable in origin. The exception to this is fish, whose fat is also polyunsaturated. These vegetable oils are liquid at room temperature. The best of these to produce the cholesterol-lowering effect are corn oil, safflower oil, sunflower oil, cottonseed oil, and soybean oil.

"Remember, different vegetable oils contain different degrees of polyunsaturation. The more unsaturated, the better."

"What about margarine?" Evelyn asked. "What is the difference in tub margarine and stick margarine?"

"Just like vegetable oils," Dr. Clement replied, "they differ in the degree of saturation. The harder the margarine, the more saturated it is. Therefore, as a rule of thumb, the softer, the better. Tub is better than stick."

"Would you go over again a simplified way of reducing our fat intake and which fats to cut down on?" Evelyn wanted to make sure she had all the basics on this part of her diet.

"Okay," Dr. Clement responded, "let me give you a quick review to plant in your mind firmly the importance of cutting fat from your diet and how to do it.

"You remember I said that the average American takes about 40 percent of his or her calories in the form of fat. Many overweight Americans take easily 50 percent of their caloric intake from fats. Most new diets instruct you to cut your caloric intake from this 45 percent range from fat to 20 to 30 percent. Personally, I don't think many people can or will keep up with their caloric intake of fat that closely. Therefore, we encourage you to forget percentage points and concentrate on cutting down on all fats as much as possible for two reasons. First, all fat is high in calories, and no matter how much average Americans try to cut down on fats, they still tend to eat too much fat. We want you to eliminate that problem.

"Second, saturated fats will increase your LDL-C, and you don't want that increase because that cholesterol is atherosclerotic as it deposits on the walls of arteries."

"So you're saying saturated fats are considered as bad for you as cholesterol?" Andy asked.

"Yes. Indirectly, saturated fats should be thought of in the same way as cholesterol since they do cause an increase in cholesterol. That's a good way to look at it—perhaps not equal to cholesterol but certainly in the same category. I want to stress the significance of saturated fats, and I want you to realize that it isn't dietary cholesterol alone causing all the problem; saturated fat is cholesterol's first cousin. You just need to learn the basic foods containing these saturated fats."

"Go over those foods one more time in a little more detail," pleaded Andy.

"Think mainly of beef when thinking meat, but saturated fat is also in pork and lamb. As a matter of fact, it is in all meats of animal origin. So, think beef, then butter and cream and whole milk. Remember these four foods because the majority of the fat in them is saturated.

"There are also a few vegetable fats that you must remember. Three fats from vegetables are a significant source of fatty acids: coconut, palm, and cocoa butter, which is in the chocolate you like so much."

■ You are not retaining water, you're fat.

"I'm becoming slightly confused about which meats to eat and which to avoid," Andy again interrupted. "Could you give us a guideline to go by for choosing meats?"

"Sure. We'll go over a chart that explains what I'm talking about in the relationship between saturated fats and cholesterol." Dr. Clement pulled a chart from his desk and showed it to the couple.

One Ounce	Saturated Fat (grams)	Cholesterol (milligrams)
Beef	1.3–4.8	27
Lamb	1.0–3.6	28
Pork	1.0–2.5	25
Chicken, with skin	1.2	25
Chicken, dark, skinless	0.5	26
Chicken, light, skinless	0.4	22
Fish: Flounder	0.0	14

"As you can see, all those meats listed have a similar amount of cholesterol except the fish. However, the amount of saturated fats varies dramatically. This is a good list to memorize as a benchmark for deciding what meat to eat. Look back at the similar list of foods I made for you earlier for ranking cholesterol content only. Now you can understand the importance of saturated fat when you're deciding which meats to eat.

"As you can see by the list, beef has up to ten times more saturated fat than skinless light chicken. Remember this fact the next time you see a beef ad stating that beef has very little more cholesterol than chicken. That ad will never point out that beef has up to ten times more saturated fat than chicken. Eating saturated fat raises your blood-cholesterol the same as eating cholesterol. It is imperative that you realize the importance of avoiding saturated fat, just as you avoid cholesterol."

Evelyn copied the list down on her pad. "This list puts it into proper perspective. I now can see why there is such a significant difference between beef and chicken.

"Avoid all fats," she wrote down. "Now, would you mind saying a little more about the difference in animal fats and vegetable fats?"

"Okay, quick review.

"Most animal fats contain a high percentage of saturated fat, which raises your LDL-cholesterol. Vegetable fats contain mostly unsaturated fats of the monounsaturated and the polyunsaturated types. You recall there are three main exceptions to vegetable oils being unsaturated—learn these three and avoid them: coconut oil and palm oil are highly saturated."

"You said three," Andy reminded Dr. Clement.

"Yes, I want to emphasize the third one separately. The third is such a favorite of most all Americans that it's easy to block it out of your mind. We think of it as high in calories, but we don't realize it can also help raise our LDL-cholesterol. I'll tell you one last time, the third saturated vegetable fat is *chocolate*."

"A double negative," exclaimed Evelyn, "calories plus saturated fat! And you say we should think of saturated fats in the same category as cholesterol when it comes to our arteries?"

"You're on target," Dr. Clement agreed. "Most studies show an increased risk of arteriosclerosis when we eat diets of not only cholesterol, but also saturated fats that are found in the four foods I told you to memorize: beef, butter, cream, and whole milk. Plus the three vegetable fats I just mentioned: chocolate, coconut oil, and palm oil."

"How did you say saturated fats increase our cholesterol count?" Andy had become more curious about the physiology of saturated fats.

"One way we think saturated fats increase cholesterol is by stimulating the liver to produce more LDL-cholesterol, the main carrier of cholesterol. Therefore, the more saturated fat, the more LDL-cholesterol.

"One more additional fact about vegetable oils. If they are hydrogenated—that's written on the product—they are much more saturated."

"That's about all I can cram into my brain concerning saturated fats." Andy was calling time out.

"You're right," Dr. Clement responded, "enough is enough. If you review what we've gone over and get it firmly in your mind, that will be plenty for your diet as recommended by the Save Your Life Cholesterol Plan.

"Here's a practical way to cut out the fats from your diets." Dr. Clement began to write a list on his pad.

Five Categories to Avoid:

1. RED MEAT. Think fish and skinless chicken instead of beef, lamb, and pork.
2. FRIED FOODS. Think baked or broiled meats instead.
3. BAKED FOODS. Remember the next time you look in the window of a bakery, about one-half of the calories you are looking at is derived from fat. Put chocolate in this category of baked goods.
4. DAIRY PRODUCTS. Dairy products have high fat contents. These are your cheeses, whole milk, and ice cream.
5. FATTY CONDIMENTS. Fatty condiments such as butter, margarine, mayonnaise, and salad dressings should be used sparingly or left off completely.

"Memorize these five categories. Practice avoiding these foods until it becomes habit not to order french fries, to order chicken or fish instead of steak, until you don't crave those little baked cakes you keep a supply of in your kitchen drawer, until you avoid ice cream and cheese like the plague, and until you find a good low-calorie dressing you like and pass up the butter and mayonnaise completely.

"I think you can take what we've gone over and develop your new diet in an intelligent, orderly fashion. You now know what fat, especially saturated fat, does from a caloric standpoint and from a cholesterol standpoint. I will conclude with that statement. Good luck."

"Would you mind if I summarize what I got out of our visit with you?" Andy looked at his notes.

"Go right ahead," Dr. Clement replied. "I'd like to hear it."

"Okay," he began. "First you explained that coronary heart disease is the number one killer of both men and women and that the basis of coronary heart disease is simply the plugging up of the arteries to the heart and one of the major plugs is cholesterol."

"You're on the right track," Dr. Clement encouraged him. "Go ahead."

"You went on to say that this part of dieting would not necessarily make us lose weight but was every bit as important because it could make us live longer."

"So far, so good."

"You mentioned three main risk factors that cause people to develop heart attacks."

"I like that expression, 'develop heart attacks,'" Dr. Clement interrupted. "Most people think they simply 'have a heart attack.' You are absolutely right. People 'develop' coronary heart disease. That process is called the *cholesterol syndrome*. Go ahead with the three main risk factors."

"Well, you first said that our genes play a role, but we can't control our ancestors. The three things you did mention were cigarette smoking, high blood pressure, and the cholesterol in our blood."

"Great!" responded Dr. Clement. "Keep going."

"You said that most of us know our blood pressure level, but very few of us know our cholesterol level and we need to find that out."

"And what about the types of cholesterol?" Dr. Clement interjected.

"The bad cholesterol is the low-density lipoprotein-cholesterol or LDL-C; and the good cholesterol is the high-density lipoprotein-cholesterol, HDL-C," Andy continued. "We need to avoid LDL-C and try to elevate our HDL-C."

■ *Only one in five hundred Americans has a genetic defect that affects the LDL-cholesterol receptors in his or her body.*

"And how do you do this?" the doctor asked.

"You avoid fats in your diet to control your LDL-C and exercise to elevate your HDL-C. You also mentioned the importance of the ratio of these two cholesterols to each other.

"And finally, you stressed the importance of saturated fats in relationship to cholesterol. I now know which meats and which three vegetable fats are high in saturated fats."

The doctor closed his notebook. "I think you're both ready to begin your life-style dieting. Now, I'm going to send you on to Dr. Shaw. He will take you into more detail about the way to live out this knowledge so that it becomes second nature with you. He will lead you to action in your eating habits. You're going to enjoy Dr. Shaw."

Andy and Evelyn left Dr. Clement's office with the foundation they needed to build a life-style change in their diets for the rest of their lives. They can fulfill their dreams of having healthy bodies.

4

THE PHYSIOLOGY OF CHOLESTEROL IN THE HUMAN BODY

Dr. Jake Shaw is a pleasant gentleman with a sense of presence about him. He has a trim physique and gentle manner. The first impression he made was such that Andy and Evelyn instantly liked him.

Dr. Shaw greeted them with an outstretched hand. "I want to welcome you to the Save Your Life Cholesterol Plan. I think what we have to discuss today will be very interesting to you both. Have a seat and we'll get right into the matter." He motioned them to sit in two comfortably padded chairs directly in front of his desk. On the arm of each chair were a legal pad and a pen for taking notes. He wanted them to take lots of notes.

"Before we get under way, I want to relate what I heard on a recording several years ago. This speaker maintained that if you are an executive and more than fifteen pounds overweight, every additional pound of weight beyond the fifteen costs you a thousand dollars per year in income. The upper echelons of management, the top corporate executives, are almost never obese. You seldom see one who smokes or who has a drinking or drug problem. The climbers maybe, but the ones at the very top have gotten there by maintaining the life-style we're talking about in the Save Your Life Cholesterol Plan. You can easily understand we're talking about more than dieting here. We're not going to affect only your weight; we'll touch many aspects of your life. It's going to be exciting; just wait and see the difference when it's all over.

"We, in America, have one of the longest life expectancies in the world; yet many of us still die prematurely because of our diet. America stands out as a wealthy country. Our high socio-economic level has enabled us to afford the foods rich in cholesterol. Our objective with this diet program is to get the word out that you can be your best, can reach your full potential of living by accepting what we have to offer: new eating habits for life."

"I know my diet habits are terrible," said Andy. "They have been for years."

"We want to persuade you that your health is the most important commodity you have in this world and then show you how to protect your health with a permanent change in that eating life-style." Dr. Shaw spoke in a serious tone. He offered no jokes, no small talk—just the facts concerning the most important medical benefit available to the general public in this decade. "How would you sum up your everyday eating style?" He looked at Andy.

"I'll start with lunch. It used to be a Wendy's double all the way with cheese and a large order of fries. That was after a big breakfast at home, consisting of a couple of eggs and some bacon. I really liked country ham when I could talk my wife into cooking it. I didn't want my toast fixed in a toaster and then buttered. I liked it toasted in the oven with lots of squares of butter on it—you know, so the butter would melt down into the bread. It would not be uncommon for me to eat three or four pieces of toast with jelly. Anything with cheese was a favorite. I liked butter on potatoes, bread, peas; almost anything tastes better with butter on it. As a matter of fact, any dairy product tastes good to me."

"That's typical," responded Dr. Shaw. "We have to lay to rest the infamous idea that the all-American breakfast should consist of bacon, eggs, buttered toast, and a glass of milk."

"Dr. Clement said coronary heart disease is our biggest enemy. How bad a problem do you think it really is?" Evelyn was concerned for the first time in her life about the fact that being overweight could actually take years off her life.

■ *High blood cholesterol: one of the main causes of the number one killer in America.*

"I'll tell you just how serious that problem is," Dr. Shaw said emphatically. "In the United States over a million people a year have heart attacks from having plugged-up arteries in their hearts. A third of these attacks will prove fatal. Coronary heart disease is the largest cause of deaths in the United States. You are developing coronary heart disease right now and don't even realize it. Most individuals want to diet to lose weight. We feel that everyone should diet to develop healthy eating habits that will prevent this number one killer disease from silently attacking our arteries every day. Much of what we eat is deposited into the walls of our arteries until finally, there is a blockage, and that silent disease suddenly becomes a massive heart attack.

"The main cause of this blockage of the arteries is cholesterol. You can prevent this disease, and that is what we want to teach you. We want your blood-cholesterol to drop by 15 to 20 percent and decrease significantly your chances of having a heart attack. You see, we have studied the overall problem of coronary heart disease methodologically, and we know what the average individual eats. We are out to change the eating habits of as many Americans as will follow our program."

"There goes my all-American diet," Andy shrugged his shoulders.

"That's right," Dr. Shaw smiled. "We'll have you eating less cholesterol, saturated fats, alcohol, total fats, and total calories. You'll be eating more complex carbohydrates and fiber, and increasing the amounts of cereals, fruits, and vegetables you consume."

"That's what I want to know—what to eat and not to eat," Evelyn said. "I'm just not sure what the problem is when it comes to the specific foods I eat every day."

"That's what the Save Your Life Cholesterol Plan is all about," Dr. Shaw explained. "Too few Americans know the problem. We want to get the news out in a way that people will understand and then be motivated to change their ways of eating. Most Americans think it's important to lose weight; but it's even more important to eat the proper foods as you lose that weight. Then we will encourage you to continue eating those same foods to protect the arteries in your body, specifically the arteries in your heart."

"You really have gotten me interested in my arteries, Dr. Shaw. Can you explain to us how cholesterol actually causes blockage?" Andy had developed a real desire about this second aspect of dieting—the preventive and protective features. Some of his friends who are not so old have already had their first heart attack. Losing his excess weight was not much of a challenge to him since he had set his goals, but this artery problem with cholesterol was something else. He wanted that ounce of prevention.

"Okay, let's talk about the physiology of blocked arteries. You have already heard that the three greatest risk factors for coronary heart disease are smoking, high blood pressure, and elevated cholesterol since they are the causative factors in blockage of the arteries. We will center on how cholesterol and its related culprit, saturated fats, affect the walls of arteries."

"What about genetics?" Evelyn asked. "I heard that a lot of the heart attack problem was due to your genes."

"True," Dr. Shaw agreed, "but it's a very small factor. In an American Heart Association Nutrition Committee report, published in the journal *Circulation*, we find genetic factors do indeed play a role in elevating cholesterol in some individuals. They point out that plasma LDL-cholesterol concentration may be elevated due to one's genes and that genetic factors probably are the cause in individuals whose LDL-C falls in the top 5 to 10 percent of everyone tested. Such individuals may require drug therapy in addition to diet changes. So, even if you have a hereditary disorder, you still need to work at eating less cholesterol in addition to taking medication for your elevated cholesterol. That is one reason you should have your cholesterol tested, and if it is elevated, let your physician determine whether you need medication in addition to changing your diet.

"Although genes do play an important role in determining how your body responds to the cholesterol you eat, the most significant factors concerning coronary heart disease and elevated cholesterol levels are the foods we eat. The big ones are meat, eggs, cheese, and butter. Remember those four categories of food, and you have started on the road to life-style eating."

"In other words," Andy responded, "people who eat foods high in cholesterol and saturated fat are more likely to develop blockages in their arteries than those who don't?"

"That's putting it fairly simply, but correctly," Dr. Shaw pointed out. "Look at groups of people in different parts of the world who eat lots of cholesterol and compare them with those who eat little cholesterol. Compare their rates of coronary heart disease and your eyes will be opened to a problem you didn't know existed. Take for example the people of Finland. They eat the greatest amount of fat in the whole world, resulting in the highest cholesterol level and also the largest number of citizens with heart disease per capita. The United States ranks second in those same categories. But in Japan, where the average diet has very little cholesterol, coronary heart disease is rare."

"Okay," Andy interrupted, "what would happen if you took someone from Japan and moved him to America and fed him the typical American diet?"

"His incidence of blocked arteries and coronary heart disease would increase dramatically." Dr. Shaw went on. "Facts concerning that very question have been reported in two articles in the *American Journal of Cardiology*. First, the material collected showed a high correlation between the amount of calories taken in as saturated fats and the rise in cholesterol. The study showed that Japanese who moved to San Francisco have a 21 percent higher cholesterol count than their counterparts living in Japan. It also showed that death rates from coronary heart disease were 2.8 times greater for the Japanese living in San Francisco than for Japanese living in Japan.

"The genetic makeup is similar between the Japanese living in Japan and those in San Francisco. Therefore, the increase in saturated fats and cholesterol in their diet is playing a significant role in their elevated cholesterol and increased death rate from coronary heart disease.

"This scenario wasn't included in the report, but I can tell you what probably happened. The diet change for the Japanese living in San Francisco was probably very subtle, very elusive initially. It probably involved no more than an egg a week and a pat of butter a week on some bread. The weeks extended into years and they acquired the taste for more foods containing cholesterol. As their diet changed in the Western world, the plaque of cholesterol began to build up in their arteries. No big deal—just a little bacon here, a hamburger there, a new-tasting omelette, a dish of ice cream at night during the summer months. These Japanese knew no more about what cholesterol was doing to them than most Americans know today.

"These and other studies have been fairly uniform in showing that there definitely is a decreased risk of coronary heart disease with diets that lower the cholesterol in our blood. Furthermore, no population has been reported to have a high rate of coronary heart disease and low blood-cholesterol."

"That is very convincing evidence. So what foods work against having coronary heart disease?" Evelyn asked a pertinent question.

"By looking at the diets of people in third world countries where there is very little coronary heart disease, we see what foods are safe: the complex carbohydrates, starches and fiber, and vegetable protein rather than animal protein.

■ *Americans have one of the highest cholesterol levels in the world. Americans have one of the highest heart attack rates in the world.*

"I have done extensive travel in places such as Africa, Bangladesh, and New Guinea where the diets are completely different from what we find in America. Those people eat very few foods with cholesterol and saturated fat. They eat lots of rice and carbohydrates. I was in the jungles of New Guinea and found approximately 90 percent of their diet consisted of sweet potatoes plus a type of root they grind into paste. That is all they eat. I perform vascular surgery here in the States, but I didn't have to operate on any arteries there. They had no blockage of their arteries; no atherosclerosis was to be found because they don't eat the cholesterol that causes the blockage.

"The same is true in Africa where cornmeal or a special root is ground and mixed into a paste. The same in Bangladesh where so much rice is eaten. No arterial operations to be done here either. No coronary heart disease is found except in nations that have become affluent enough to start eating Western foods. We will be wise to look at diets of these third world countries and become more aware of their intrinsic values for a healthy body."

"You're saying eat less fat and more complex carbohydrates, vegetables, and fiber like these nationals do. I'm beginning to get the picture. But you were going to explain how the arteries become blocked," Andy reminded Dr. Shaw.

Dr. Shaw picked up a pad of paper and drew an artery with thickened walls.

"You both remember the two basic types of cholesterol?"

"Yes, the bad type is the low-density lipoprotein you call LDL-C," Evelyn replied.

"And the good guy is the HDL-C, the high-density lipoprotein," Andy added.

"Right," Dr. Shaw agreed. "Most of the cholesterol we eat is the LDL-C type—the bad type." He pointed to the drawing showing particles of LDL-C embedded in the arterial wall. "LDL-C is bombarded against the lining of the artery, breaks through, and actually gets stuck in the substance of the wall.

"The HDL-C also flows into the wall of arteries but somehow is able to exit. The actual physiology of how it works isn't completely known, but HDL-C is presumed to act as a scavenger and clear the cholesterol that is already lodged in the wall. HDL-C may actually incorporate cholesterol into its central core and then transport it to the liver to be excreted."

"So the cholesterol keeps building up in the wall of the artery until it clogs the entire opening of the artery?" Andy asked.

"Exactly," Dr. Shaw responded. "It takes years to do, but the more cholesterol we eat, the more enters into the arterial walls."

"And if it blocks the arteries in the heart, you have a heart attack?" Andy had drawn the right conclusion.

"And if it blocks the arteries in the brain, you have a stroke," Dr. Shaw added.

Andy thought a few seconds before asking the next question. "Doctor, if the same process blocked the arteries to your male sex organs, would that make you impotent? You know, as you get older?"

"Yes, blocked arteries are a major contributor to the problem of impotency, but not a lot is said about it," Dr. Shaw replied. "Arteriosclerosis is a generalized disease that can affect any artery in the body including those to your sex organs. Arteries going to different organs are blocked by this disease and cause different problems as a result of that blockage. We speak mostly about the arteries feeding the muscles in the heart because such blockage is dramatic and so common. The same process found in the arteries in the neck deprives blood from the brain, resulting in a stroke. Blocked arteries going to the lower extremities result in severe cramping pains in the calf muscles. A deposit of cholesterol in the arteries going to the kidneys as well as a generalized deposit throughout the arteries of the body can result in hypertension. A depositing of cholesterol means serious consequences when you're dealing with such vital parts of the body."

"What you're saying is enough reason for me to follow your diet," Andy said. "Keep talking."

"Now do you understand why cholesterol is so bad for you?" Dr. Shaw asked.

"You've convinced me!" Evelyn's voice conveyed her understanding. "Dr. Clement mentioned saturated fats earlier. How much importance do you place on them?" she continued.

"He's right. Cholesterol that you eat is not the only factor related to damaging the walls of arteries and causing arteriosclerosis," Dr. Shaw replied. "Diets high in saturated fat that is found in most meats and dairy products plus three vegetable fats: coconut oil, palm oil, and chocolate—all increase the problem of hardening of the arteries by secondarily raising your cholesterol.

"They are important to avoid," Dr. Shaw continued, "but for simplicity, we will tell you the foods to avoid with a cholesterol or a cholesterol-saturated fat combination. We'll go into that in more detail later. Right now, just try to realize that the amounts of cholesterol and saturated fat that you take in have a direct effect on the concentration of cholesterol and LDL-C; and the higher the concentration of cholesterol in the blood, the more it will impact the walls of arteries."

"I understand that women have fewer heart attacks than men," Evelyn remembered. "Is that related to this LDL-C you're talking about?"

"Yes," Dr. Shaw nodded his head. "There are factors other than what you eat that affect HDL-C and LDL-C, and one of those is being a male or female. Usually, men have less of the protective HDL-C than women; and men usually have more of the LDL-C than women. That is believed to be one of the reasons there are 60 percent fewer heart attacks among women than men."

"What about exercise and HDL-C?" Andy wanted Dr. Shaw to continue his lesson since he was beginning to understand about the specifics of cholesterol.

"Another doctor will go into the specifics of HDL-C and exercise, but I'll give you a little thought to nibble on about the protective effect of HDL-C versus the harmful effect of LDL-C and how they relate to exercise," Dr. Shaw said.

"Exercise has been proven to raise the protective HDL-C level in humans. However, there's still a question about just how much exercise is necessary to raise this level significantly.

"But the Lipid Research Clinics Primary Prevention Trial pointed out the one factor we're sure of, and that is the direct correlation between the amount of cholesterol in blood and the danger of heart attacks. Many studies have shown that for every percent reduction in blood-cholesterol, there is a 2 percent reduction in coronary heart disease. The National Institutes of Health has published results of a clinical trial showing beyond doubt that men who reduced their elevated blood-cholesterol experienced fewer heart attacks than did men whose cholesterol remained at a high level. In fact, the men who reduced their cholesterol by 25 percent cut their risk of heart attack by half." Dr. Shaw restated how important lowering blood-cholesterol is.

"I've heard that the protein in red meat is bad for us," Andy interjected, "but I've also heard that some red meat doesn't have all that much cholesterol. Could you explain why meat protein is so bad for you?"

"Well, one way to look at it is to realize animal protein contains both cholesterol and saturated fat, while vegetable protein is low in fat content. So, red meat hits you from both sides while vegetable proteins are high in fiber and complex carbohydrates."

■ *Even after a heart attack, lowering your blood cholesterol is effective in preventing a second such attack.*

"Could we summarize from what you have said," Evelyn looked back at her notes, "that if we lower the amount of cholesterol and saturated fat in our diet, we will lower the particles of cholesterol in our blood and, in turn, decrease the amount of cholesterol lodging in the walls of our arteries and finally lower our risk of having a heart attack?"

"You get an A+ for that summation," Dr. Shaw said. "I think I've succeeded in getting my point across to you. I know that both of you will change your eating life-style once you realize the benefits of the Save Your Life Cholesterol Plan.

"Before I finish my time with you, I'd like to emphasize that you're not going to take care of your body physically until you're sold on the idea psychologically. You have to realize the importance of motivation in this program. You can't compartmentalize your thinking and your actions. You can't motivate yourself to diet and exercise without becoming motivated in every aspect of your life.

"Take Dr. Clement's advice about listening to tapes seriously. If you don't have a cassette tape player in your automobile, buy one today and put it in. Get some educational and motivating tapes to play while you travel. It's remarkable the amount of time we spend in our cars by ourselves. Utilize that time as motivational time. Make your automobile a library. There is a wealth of literature and information on tapes. Invest in yourself. Work on your attitude. Listen to information that will give you the positive attitude it takes to become successful in the Save Your Life Cholesterol Plan. At the same time, you will become successful in life itself.

"I believe you're ready now for the specifics of the Save Your Life Cholesterol Plan. You may have noticed that each doctor you talk to overlaps somewhat with what the other doctors on the team are telling you. The reasons for this are twofold: first, repetition increases the significance of certain aspects of the program; second, the overall program is so integrated that the separate parts cannot be talked about completely independently.

"I want you to proceed to Dr. Patricia Holly's office where you will receive some specifics to implement at once. You are now ready for action, so take hold of your hat and be prepared for some knowledge that will change your life by changing how you eat the rest of your days. I wish you well."

5

How to WANT to Eat Differently

The couple walked next into the office of Dr. Patricia Holly. She was attractive, dressed sharply, and certainly didn't need to lose any weight. She welcomed them into her office and gave each a pad of paper and a pen to take notes during her session.

"I'm to review some of the basic concepts of the Save Your Life Cholesterol Plan with you and help you set the specific goals Dr. William Franklin taught you in your first session," Dr. Holly began. "I realize you came to us to lose excess weight, and that is going to be our primary objective. We also want to ground you in what food to eat while you're losing your weight. When you reach your desired weight, you'll already have the proper eating habits to protect you against the probable cause of your death—coronary heart disease."

"That's eerie—to think about dying from diseased arteries of my heart. When you make it so personal, I listen. We already realize you are talking about two subjects. One is losing weight, and one is learning what to eat to protect the arteries in our hearts. Are we going to have to learn two different diets?" Andy wondered if the program would get too complex to follow.

"No, same diet, different quantities," Dr. Holly responded. "We'll teach you the right foods to eat and then throw two pitches at you. First will be quantity; you'll be strictly limited to the number of calories you should eat during the weight-loss period. Second, exercise. We'll devise an exercise program that will be fun for you and suited to your personality."

"I'm not worried about my personality," Andy said. "I just don't particularly like wasting my time exercising."

"That's what I'm talking about," Dr. Holly smiled. "We'll plan your exercise around the fact that you don't want to waste any time while you're exercising. We'll have you doing something you think is productive while you're exercising.

"Now, let's get on with what your goals ought to be on this diet. Do you remember the basic goal structure Dr. Franklin taught you in the first session?"

"Sure. What are our major goals?" Andy picked up the pen and pad. He clearly remembered the breakdown of goals.

"The major goal is a three-part goal," Dr. Holly said. "One, to decrease the amount of cholesterol we eat. Two, to decrease the amount of total fat and saturated fat we eat. And three, to drastically increase the amount of complex carbohydrates and fiber in our diets."

"Cholesterol, fats, carbohydrates," Andy repeated. "Are these broken down into intermediate goals?"

"How did you guess?" Dr. Holly continued. "Take the cholesterol. Your intermediate goal is to eliminate all egg yolks and organ meats; to limit meat intake to four ounces of red meat, fish, or poultry per day, eating red meat only occasionally; and to eliminate butter by using tub margarine.

"For the intermediate goal in the fat and saturated fats portion you need to avoid fried foods and cheeses, eliminate mayonnaise, avoid salad dressings, use low-fat milk, and avoid coconut oil, palm oil, and chocolate.

"And last, the complex carbohydrate part of the goal: eat two to four servings of complex carbohydrates at each meal. They include breads, potatoes, beans, vegetables, pasta, and cereal. These are the foods that will fill you up, and they need to become the major portion of your diet. This portion of your diet will guarantee complete satiety because of the volume of food you will be able to eat."

"What about the immediate action goals?" Andy continued to take notes. "How do they fit into all this?"

"The immediate action goals in this diet structure are based on what single factor?" Dr. Holly looked toward Evelyn.

She already had this in mind. "Right now," she said quickly, "the immediate action goals depend on what we do about what you've taught us today—not tomorrow."

"Exactly," responded Dr. Holly. "Right now, you have to put this plan into effect. Right now, you don't eat that chocolate chip cookie when you leave here. Right now, you stop by the grocery store and buy 1 or 2 percent milk. Right now, you throw away the butter in your refrigerator and buy some tub margarine. Right now, you eat a piece of fruit for your next snack rather than cookies or cake. Right now, you begin to eat meat at only one meal a day and zero in on fish and poultry. Right now, you stop ordering cheese and mayonnaise on any sandwich. Right now, you decide you are going to develop the best body you can with what's given you to work with. You want to be trim. You want to look great. Right now, you are successful at becoming a new you."

"That's exciting!" Andy exclaimed. "How about going over some of the details of the goals you have outlined and give us some recommendations we can start working on."

"You can start with reduction and substitution of the foods we just mentioned." Dr. Holly began her review. "Begin to concentrate on cholesterol. Look at it as the one substance, more than any other, that blocks the walls of arteries. Begin to visualize what happens to that butter on your potato or bread once it enters your digestive tract and then your bloodstream. Begin to see that particle of cholesterol encased in low-density lipoprotein finding its way into the wall of one of your arteries of your heart. Begin to realize that every little particle that lodges in the wall adds to the cholesterol you have eaten over the years. Once you really begin to visualize in your mind what's taking place in your body, then eating that bite of butter isn't all that much fun anymore. Suddenly, those two words, *heart attack*, begin to flash in your mind every once in a while.

■ The cornerstone of treatment for controlling cholesterol: diet.

"I have patients who come to me with lung problems. I instruct them to quit smoking. I would say that 99 percent of the patients who quit smoking for good are the ones who throw away the cigarettes in their pockets at that moment and never smoke another one. Very few people can cut down on the number of cigarettes and then gradually quit.

"It's the same way with certain foods. Some, you just have to decide *right now* that you're not going to eat anymore. Butter is one of those foods. Margarine contains fat but no cholesterol. I simply advise not eating any more butter. Eggs are another such food simply to quit. Just don't order eggs for breakfast anymore. At least don't eat any yolks. That's where the cholesterol is. Personally, I was able to quit butter and eggs all at once—*right now.*"

"Can I gradually change other portions of my diet?" Evelyn asked. "I know I can't change all my eating habits at once."

"Some habits will change gradually," Dr. Holly admitted. "But I would not plan it that way. I advise you to start right now, while you are motivated, to eliminate the bad foods and substitute the foods we recommend. You have to lay a foundation for a habit sometime, and the best time is when you *first* hear about a particular food or change. Procrastination will kill the effect of a great ambition.

"Limit or eliminate sausage and bacon at breakfast. Begin to look for lite cheese if you feel you want cheese. Think of egg yolk as poison. Eat fish or chicken instead of red meat. Order a baked potato rather than french fries. Begin to eat more and more meals completely without meat; use soups, salads, beans, and vegetables instead. Begin eating fresh fruit with your meals and for snacks."

"So you emphasize replacing one food with another," Evelyn noted.

"In one sense, yes," Dr. Holly replied. "Remember that cholesterol is found ubiquitously in animal cells, so we want to cut down on the animal products we eat. We want to eat three or four pieces of fruit a day. We want to increase the amount of vegetables to two or three servings a day. Increase the amount of beans to two to three times a week. And work hard to eliminate the fats in cooking; use only pure vegetable oils."

"I can see now that my habits are going to have to change." Andy looked at Dr. Holly. "At one time, it was not unusual to eat meat every day—usually two meals, sometimes three if we had bacon for breakfast. I like eggs. Cheese is a favorite of mine. I put butter on everything. Evelyn puts a pat of butter right on top of the creamed potatoes. I could eat ice cream every night before going to bed. These are my lifelong habits, but I see that they need to change. I want to experience that premium life that can come only through good health."

"Let me point out something of interest I found in my study of habits: bad habits sneak up on you. Nobody sets out to be a drunkard or a drug addict or to be forty pounds overweight. But little by little, bite by bite, people get there. But you gotta grab good habits. You've got to grab them right now, and that's the emphasis I want to stress—*right now*. Do it today. Do it *right now*. If you have a bad eating habit, change it *right now*.

"Habits can change," Dr. Holly continued. "And the best way to change eating habits is to become informed about what you are eating."

"I think that's helped me want to change my eating habits," Evelyn chimed in. "Just knowing what foods I ought to be eating makes a big difference. I wish you would go over some of the specific foods to emphasize their importance in our diets."

"Gladly," Dr. Holly began. "Let's take meats in general. All three of the bad factors—cholesterol, fats, and saturated fats—are major components in meats. One fact to remember is that organ meats are very high in cholesterol. Don't eat organ meats, period!"

"That's easy for me," Andy joked. "I never did like liver or gizzards or brains."

"Any meat you do eat has fat on the outside, which you can trim, but also fat on the inside, which you don't see," continued Dr. Holly. "Remember, even in eating chicken, there is a significant amount of fat just under the skin; so remove the skin. Begin to replace higher fat meat, such as beef, lamb, and pork, with fish and chicken, and at the same time, begin to cut down on the number of times you eat meat.

"Look at red meat, cheese, and eggs as equal culprits. Don't have eggs for breakfast, and try lunches without meat or cheese. Begin to concentrate more on cereals, soups, salads, fruits, breads, and beans."

"What about cheeses?" Evelyn was still making notes.

"Think of cheeses as interchangeable with meat," Dr. Holly replied. "The cholesterol and saturated fat in egg yolks, cheese, and red meat, are about the same and in that order with egg yolks being the worst. So, think of cheese as something to avoid. Avoid it on hamburgers, avoid it on sandwiches, avoid it as snacks."

"But I cook with cheese so much of the time," Evelyn exclaimed.

"I know. Americans eat large quantities of high-fat cheese," Dr. Holly agreed. "But you can cut the problem about one-third by being selective in the cheese you buy. There are more and more reduced-calorie, reduced-fat cheeses. Sealtest has such cheeses, and Borden's Lite-Line and Hickory Farms' Lyte are good choices. If you're going to eat cheese, at least be selective in what you buy."

"You keep talking about egg yolks," said Andy. "How bad are they really?"

■ *Five foods that make up 90 percent of the cholesterol you eat, in order of consumption: (1) egg yolk, (2) red meat, (3) whole milk, (4) cheese, and (5) butter.*

"Egg yolks are the greatest single source of the cholesterol we eat. About 40 percent of all the cholesterol we eat comes from egg yolks, and about one-half of that is from eating eggs directly and the other half from eggs mixed in other foods. So you can see with some easy arithmetic we can cut our total cholesterol approximately 20 percent by cutting out eggs at breakfast. As far as using eggs in cooking, Evelyn can start using two egg whites for every whole egg a recipe calls for. An additional 20 percent of our cholesterol comes from dairy products—milk, cheese, and butter. Start drinking 2 percent, then 1 percent milk, perhaps even skim milk. I've told you how buying the right type cheese can cut your cholesterol and fat one-third. And we have already reviewed eliminating butter. That leaves only ice cream, which you can replace with no-fat frozen yogurt or sherbet."

"So, 60 percent of the cholesterol we're eating now is from

egg yolks and dairy products." Andy had added the percentages together. "Where does the other 40 percent come from?"

"The remainder of our cholesterol comes mainly from red meats, which makes up about 30 percent of all the cholesterol we eat. The other 10 percent also comes from meat: poultry and fish. You can easily understand the need to cut down drastically on red meat if you are to cut down on your cholesterol."

"Like you said—eggs, dairy products, and red meat." Andy referred to his notes. "I'll think of these whenever I think of cholesterol."

Cholesterol We Eat

Eggs	40%
Red Meat	30%
Dairy	20%

Andy jotted down his own little chart to envision where his cholesterol was coming from. "You doctors have taught me to visualize what's going on in my arteries when I eat cholesterol. Now I'm going to make a mental picture of the foods with cholesterol. Whenever I hear the word *cholesterol*, I'm going to see a big steak with a slice of cheese melting down the sides of that steak, and right on top of the cheese is a fried egg with the yellow broken and running down over the cheese. That one picture will give me the breakdown I need to remember. The egg on top—40 percent. The cheese in the middle represents milk, cheese, and butter—20 percent. And the steak representing red meat—30 percent. That's a mental picture I'll never forget.

"You also mentioned mayonnaise," Andy continued. "How do we treat mayonnaise?"

"Think of mayonnaise as fat," Dr. Holly began, "because it is about two-thirds fat. I was able to quit mayonnaise 'cold turkey.' I quit using it on sandwiches, quit ordering it on sandwiches, and I started buying the light mayonnaises to use sparingly at home, so that pretty well took care of it for me.

"The main detail to remember is that mayonnaise is mostly fat; think of it almost as butter. It has the same number of calories as butter and has almost one-third the amount of saturated fat and cholesterol as butter. With that in mind, you will most likely do without it, or at least you won't pile it on the bread when you make a sandwich."

"I've never thought of it like butter or anything else," Andy chimed in. "I've never given mayonnaise any thought at all. It's something I can take or leave, so I'll just leave it."

"You mentioned butter." Evelyn looked at Dr. Holly. "What about butter?"

"It's one food that is packed with both cholesterol and saturated fats. You must avoid it."

"But I like butter so much in cooking."

"I'm sure you do," Dr. Holly agreed, "but it's crammed full of cholesterol and saturated fats that make such a bad combination for our arteries. You must switch to a soft margarine. It's made mainly from unsaturated fat and has no cholesterol. Margarine has only about one-third of the saturated fats that butter has.

"Margarine has no cholesterol," Dr. Holly continued, "but it still has the same number of calories as fat, so you can't eat margarine in any quantity you want. It's still fattening."

"Given the choice between sour cream and margarine on my baked potato, which is better?" Andy still hadn't given up the idea that he could put *something* on his baked potato.

"Sour cream should be viewed as identical with butter in calories as well as saturated fats and cholesterol. Sour cream equals butter. If you have to have something, then use a *little* margarine. But remember, it still has just as many calories as butter, and you don't want to lose the low-calorie benefit of the baked potato by pouring on the margarine."

"Okay," Evelyn nodded her head, "I can handle the butter—I

may cheat just a little in some of my cooking—but what's your advice on milk? So far, anything that comes from cows has been bad."

"Milk is not that big a problem. Milk is considered nature's most nearly perfect food because it has more nutrients our body needs than any other food. But one component it contains that we don't need is butterfat. We advise you just to switch to 2 percent, 1 percent, or skim milk. Two percent milk is not so bad a switch from whole milk as far as taste goes." Dr. Holly was trying to simplify the milk problem.

"You talk about whole milk and 2 percent milk," Andy interrupted. "What percent fat is whole milk? How much are we cutting down if we go to 2 percent? I don't know if whole milk is 2.5 percent or 10 percent. How much are we saving by going to 2 percent?"

"Good question," Dr. Holly laughed. "Think of whole milk as being 4 percent fat. Actually, it's usually a little less, but it's easy to think of 2 percent milk being about one-half the fat and 1 percent milk being about one-fourth the fat of whole milk."

"So 1 percent would be much better for me?" Andy pressed for the strictest limits.

"No doubt," Dr. Holly agreed. "And skim milk even better. But if we're talking about a diet you're going to make a habit of eating, you have to decide where you, individually, are willing to draw the line. Personally, I don't like skim milk and don't particularly like 1 percent milk. I stick to 2 percent. Otherwise, I might cheat a little, as Evelyn said she might with the butter. I would rather set my goal realistically at 2 percent milk and not cheat. I am my own life-style. I am not a fanatic, but am interested in protecting my arteries. Just remember, skim milk is better than 2 percent. You decide. Most people drink 2 percent without any trouble. After two months, they can switch to 1 percent, and in two more months to skim."

"What about Evelyn's cheating on the butter?" Andy wanted to see exactly how Dr. Holly looked at this.

"Just be aware of what butter does to you. If a recipe calls for butter and she decides to use three-fourths margarine and one-fourth butter, then let it be. The Save Your Life Cholesterol Plan is programmed to make you aware of how bad so many of the foods are for you. Then, each of you has to decide how far you can change your diet. I'm a doctor. I treat diseases. I know it's far better to prevent a disease than to treat it. I think the Save Your Life Cholesterol Plan can do much more to help my patients prevent coronary heart disease, as well as strokes and high blood pressure, than I could ever do by giving medicines or performing operations after their arteries have hardened.

■ *The three main causes of coronary heart disease:*
(1) elevated blood cholesterol, (2) smoking, and
(3) high blood pressure.

"I personally feel that Americans are at the beginning of a mammoth change in their health. We are entering an era when Americans want the best of what health has to offer. Average health is not good enough for more and more Americans. We want the best, especially when it comes to our bodies and our health. We are realizing that the most valuable assets we own are our hearts, which pump our blood to our brains, which do our thinking; and to our legs, which do our walking. We are a more intelligent people than ten years ago. We are becoming more health conscious every day.

"Americans are waking up to the fact that we can achieve much more, reach our full potentials as individuals, if we have fit, healthy bodies. We want to know what to eat. We are realizing the benefits of exercise, in both health and productivity. Large corporations are encouraging employees to become less sedentary by furnishing exercise facilities. These corporations realize the result—increased productivity.

"I am confident the Save Your Life Cholesterol Plan can have a major impact—not only in increasing life span, but also in improving the quality of life. I think this impact will surpass the benefits of medicine I can prescribe or surgery I could perform on an individual patient. I feel the Save Your Life Cholesterol Plan is the best preventive medicine pill we can offer you today. So, we're talking about much more than hardening of the arteries. We want you to be one of the beneficiaries of a plan that gives you all the attributes of a better, healthier, fulfilled life."

"I appreciate your saying that," Andy said sincerely. "I am beginning to realize that a healthy body means more than just losing some weight on a crash diet and then regaining it in a matter of months.

"I would like to ask one other question that keeps coming up in my reading about cholesterol. What is the medical word for hardening of the arteries? I've heard of atherosclerosis and arteriosclerosis. Which is correct?"

"Both." Dr. Holly smiled again. "When you're speaking of hardening of the arteries of the heart, it's called atherosclerosis, and when you're talking about hardening of the more peripheral arteries, as in the neck or legs, it's called arteriosclerosis. Actually, the terms are used almost interchangeably since they both refer to the same process of cholesterol being laid down in arteries."

"And by hardening of the arteries," Evelyn added, "you're talking about cholesterol being deposited in the walls of the arteries, aren't you?"

"Yes, once the deposits stay awhile, they become very hard. After a few years, they can even become solid with additional calcium deposits. The walls actually become hard. If you were to open an abdomen for an operation and feel these arteries, they would feel like bone because there would be so much sclerosis from the cholesterol deposits."

"Are you going to advise us how many milligrams of cholesterol we can have a day?" Andy wanted to be exact.

"No," Dr. Holly began. "We won't make you get that detailed. What we do want you to do, though, is to develop an awareness of the amount of cholesterol you eat. If there is ever an opportunity to decrease your cholesterol intake, then seize it. If you are offered eggs or cereal for breakfast, take the cereal. If you are offered cheese to put on your sandwich, choose something else to add. In other words, we want you to become aware of what can *poison* your arteries and to want to avoid that food. We don't want you to rationalize with yourself about being entitled to a certain amount of cholesterol each day and come to the end of the day thinking you can eat that bowl of ice cream because you have part of your quota left. Our advice is to avoid all the cholesterol and saturated fats you can because there is so much hidden in foods that you could never count it all.

"We take the same approach to knowing your cholesterol level. I have a patient in the hospital who was not holding off on his cholesterol intake. He said he didn't need to because he was only five points over normal. This patient's father had recently had a heart attack; this patient was overweight and knew what the accepted normal cholesterol level was. What he didn't know was his HDL-cholesterol. The fact that his father had a heart attack places him in a higher risk category than usual. I don't want to give you any excuses to eat cholesterol. I want you to develop a diet low in saturated fats and cholesterol so that later in life, when your cholesterol tends to climb with age, you will already have the habit of eating the proper foods."

"Okay, I'll go along with that," Andy agreed. "But to give us some idea—about how much cholesterol am I eating a day, and how much should I cut out?"

"Round figures only," Dr. Holly said, "you probably average 450 to 500 milligrams of cholesterol a day. You see, two eggs for breakfast can give you almost 500 milligrams of cholesterol. The American Heart Association recommends no more than 300 milligrams a day. If you really want to try to keep track of it, I would suggest that you shoot for 100 milligrams a day."

"I see what you mean." Andy nodded. "There's no way I would know when I had eaten 100 milligrams of cholesterol or anything else. I'll just take your advice and avoid it every chance I get."

Dr. Holly concluded her session with a word of encouragement: "I challenge you to begin right now the changes we've talked about. I'm certain both of you can be successful with this program. We want to have a real impact on how you live and how you eat. The more you're informed, the more likelihood there is of your success with a low-cholesterol diet plan. We want to communicate that information.

"I'm going to send you now to Dr. Lowell Benjamin. He will take you on a different route to a good working knowledge of the Save Your Life Cholesterol Plan. You know generally what happens when you eat certain foods and they end up in your arteries. Dr. Benjamin will cover the specifics of the beginning of the cholesterol syndrome. You are going to learn a great deal about your everyday eating plan from him. I wish you both great success in your next session."

"Would you do us one favor before we leave you?" Evelyn wanted to glean a little more information from Dr. Holly.

"Sure. I'd be glad to."

"We have three children: Tom, Amy, and Elizabeth," Evelyn began. "When should we start teaching them about cholesterol? At what age does cholesterol begin to be a problem?"

"That's an excellent question." Dr. Holly became very enthusiastic. She was excited that there was spontaneous inquiry about such a practical point concerning Evelyn's family.

"I've done quite a bit of reviewing about the subject because I have a twelve-year-old myself." She pulled a stack of reprints of articles from her desk to show Evelyn and Andy.

"The one article that really made me think about when the

silent killer first begins its work of blocking the arteries of the heart was this one." Dr. Holly showed them an article entitled "Coronary Artery Disease in Combat Casualties in Vietnam" printed in the *Journal of the American Medical Association*. "The authors of the report studied 105 American soldiers killed in action in Vietnam. The coronary arteries were carefully dissected, and the degree of severity of atherosclerosis was judged. What they found astounded me. It was hard to believe what they discovered about those young soldiers."

"How old were they?" Andy interrupted.

■ *The three main dietary habits that contribute most to elevated blood cholesterol: (1) high intake of foods containing cholesterol, (2) high intake of foods containing saturated fats, and (3) a generalized high caloric intake that leads to obesity.*

"Their mean age was 22.1 years. That's what makes the study's results so pertinent to your question. They found that 45 percent of the soldiers examined had some degree of atherosclerosis in one or more of their coronary arteries. Even more alarming to me was the fact that 25 percent of them had involvement of two or more of the three main arteries of the heart."

"You have to be healthy to be in the armed services of the United States," Andy responded. "You're telling us that a lot of healthy young Americans already are setting the stage of coronary heart disease by the age of twenty-two. This process obviously begins quite some time before then. When should we become concerned about our children's cholesterol? What do the experts say about cholesterol in children?"

"That's a fair question," Dr. Holly said. "Let's look at what the American Academy of Pediatrics and other national organizations have to say about the situation.

"First, the American Academy of Pediatrics takes the stand that only children with a family history of heart disease or high cholesterol should be tested for cholesterol. In a recent issue of *Pediatrics*, a medical journal for pediatricians, the American Academy of Pediatrics' Committee on Nutrition reported that a child with a family history of either early coronary heart disease or elevated cholesterol should have a complete evaluation of cholesterol, other lipids, and lipoproteins. It does not favor testing all schoolchildren as a part of routine checkups for various reasons.

"A commentary in the *Journal of the American Medical Association* concerning cholesterol and children expressed the opinion that restriction of isolated dietary cholesterol in children was not warranted. There was question of any advantage of reducing cholesterol in the diet since membrane formation and especially nerve lipids require cholesterol. It also pointed out that cholesterol is used in hormone formation, and that fact should be taken into account when considering a cholesterol-lowering diet.

"Another report in *Pediatrics* expressed concern that there were no data related to the potential impact on growth when red meat, eggs, and dairy products were reduced in children's diet, especially during adolescence."

"It seems the American Academy of Pediatrics is fairly adamant about not screening my children for cholesterol since there is no strong family history of coronary heart disease or high cholesterol." Evelyn pondered what she should do about her children specifically. "But if there is significant evidence for cholesterol deposit in coronary arteries by age twenty-two, I think I should do something about it while my children are still growing. What do other reports indicate?"

"Other reports acknowledge that an elevated total cholesterol level is one of the strongest correlates of coronary heart disease in adults, that it seems appropriate to identify individuals who are prone to have a high cholesterol level early in life, and that prevention through dietary modification should begin in childhood and adolescence. There seems to be no doubt that the process of cholesterol being laid down in the coronary arteries starts early in life and that it is reversible if intervention is carried out before the formation of plaques, which have advanced and matured. The problem is, which children should be checked for elevated cholesterol? It was found that only about one in two hundred children has a genetic trait that gives the individual extremely high blood-cholesterol readings, but approximately 10 percent of children aged nine to ten years have blood-cholesterol levels exceeding 200 mg/dl. If we zero in on only the children whose parents have a cholesterol or heart problem, we are going to miss a lot of children who should be treated.

"One thing is for sure. We develop many habits during childhood that carry over into adulthood. Habits of diet, exercise, and weight control are all established in childhood. Once such habits, including eating habits, are formed, they are changed only with great difficulty in the adult. I like to look at the cholesterol and diet situation in light of habit formation. I think we can and should teach our children the evils of cholesterol and saturated fats and help them develop good eating habits at young ages. The genetic makeup of which children are prone to develop coronary heart disease is significant. However, if we strictly go by family risk factors to determine whether we check children's cholesterol, we will miss some who do need dietary therapy or even some who may need medication to help control their high cholesterol.

"Another article in *Pediatrics*, submitted by the Louisiana State University Medical Center in New Orleans, pointed out that the early stages of atherosclerosis begin in childhood. The researchers stated that fatty streaks of atherosclerosis begin in childhood and that fatty streaks have been found in aortas of three-year-old children. They further stated that both fatty streaks and fibrous plaques appeared in the coronary arteries during the second decade of life and were correlated with levels of fats and cholesterol fractions in the blood of children and adolescents."

"Have there been any studies where children have been tracked for long periods of time to see if a child who has an elevated cholesterol level would be more likely to carry this over into adolescence or adulthood?" Andy wanted to know if there is any correlation between cholesterol levels in his children now and later as they grow older.

"Another article in *Pediatrics* speaks to that question." Dr. Holly pulled the article from her desk. "Youngsters ages eight to eighteen were studied and then reexamined more than ten years later when their ages ranged from twenty to thirty. This report indicated that elevated levels of cholesterol during childhood were associated with a higher risk for elevated levels in adult life. In addition, it showed that obesity acquired during adolescence had detrimental effects on adult cholesterol level. It noted that total cholesterol measurements in childhood were predictors of adult LDL-cholesterol levels, with 25 to 50 percent of adult cholesterol variability explained by childhood levels."

"Do you think this correlation is related to habit formation in childhood?" Evelyn asked.

"I think that plays an important part of the cholesterol problem. Young people select the type of life-style they want to develop, and many of these selections are carried over into adulthood," Dr. Holly agreed. "We know this is true because obesity acquired in childhood is highly predictive of obesity in adult life, smoking habits are many times set by the beginning of high school, and our "all-American" eating habits that focus on foods rich in cholesterol and saturated fats are a natural among teenagers with all the fast-food restaurants and readily available snack food."

"Could you give us some type of review of what those articles showed?" Andy wanted a shortcut. "You know, right to the point."

"Okay." Dr. Holly sat down at her desk and leaned forward to keep Andy's and Evelyn's attention. "Let's start from the beginning. More than 5.4 million Americans have symptomatic coronary heart disease. That many know they have heart disease because they have chest pain or heart attacks, which tell them something is wrong with their heart. Out of that number, more than 550,000 die from coronary heart disease each year. Now, this is the point I want you to remember: millions more Americans have hidden coronary heart disease that is remaining silent. These millions are developing blockage in the arteries of their hearts and don't even know it. Both of you probably fall into this category.

"Keep with me now. The cholesterol hypothesis is stated in two parts; first, the higher the cholesterol level in your blood, the greater the incidence of coronary heart disease; and second, when the level of cholesterol in your blood is lowered, the incidence of coronary heart disease is decreased.

"You remember that 45 percent of the young soldiers in the Vietnam study showed evidence of atherosclerosis in their coronary arteries. It is highly unlikely that the process of blockage of those arteries suddenly started at the age of twenty-two.

"We spoke of fatty streaks found in children's arteries. These fatty streaks are rarely found before the age of ten but are frequently found in the second decade and are nearly always present after the age of twenty. Based on over four thousand autopsied cases from different areas of the world, a study was made of the relationship between fatty streaks and the more advanced plaques that actually cause blockage in the coronary arteries. The individuals studied were from ten to thirty-nine years of age. The conclusion was that the process began in some cases before twenty years of age and increased rapidly in the two decades that followed. Even more important was the finding that the coronary artery fatty streaks found in childhood predicted the advanced plaques of cholesterol found in middle age.

"I was at the medical meeting this past weekend where Dr. Robert Jones of Duke Medical School spoke on coronary artery disease. He is a heart surgeon who bypasses the blocked arteries of the heart. I will quote him concerning when this process of blockage of the arteries begins in life: 'Most of us start this process in our teenage years.' Here is a man who spends his life correcting a problem that begins early in life. We ought to begin teaching our children about cholesterol and saturated fats early in life.

"Now, do you remember one of the doctors telling you that citizens of countries such as the United States who had a high average level of cholesterol in the blood also had a high incidence of coronary heart disease?"

"Sure do," responded Andy.

"Well, the same was found in children," Dr. Holly continued. "The cholesterol levels of children were found to be lowest in three West African countries and in Pakistan, where coronary heart disease was also low; they were found to be highest in some European countries and the United States, where coronary heart disease was the highest.

"As you can see, there is no consensus among all physicians concerning exactly how to diagnose which children have high cholesterol nor how aggressive you should be to prevent your children from eating cholesterol and saturated fats. One thing is clear, however. Eating habits are formed to a great degree during childhood and adolescence. If the attempt to lower the cholesterol levels of the general American population is to be effective, the eating habits of the entire family must be changed. I feel you should teach your children the physiology of cholesterol in the body, show them which foods are high in cholesterol and saturated fats, and cut down on these foods eaten in abundance by the young people of America.

"I won't venture to suggest that your children should limit 30 percent or 40 percent of their diet to fat. I don't think children will have any idea what percentage of fat they are eating. But some moderation has to be taught. You have to emphasize weight control to prevent obesity in your children and help them develop good habits of exercise. They can follow a nutritious diet with adequate calories and protein for their growth and development, but can still reduce the amount of fat they are eating in fried foods and bakery foods. They can learn to reduce their cholesterol and increase the complex carbohydrates through the meals you prepare at home and what you let them order when eating out.

"Finally, should you order a serum cholesterol test on your children? I don't think there will be encouragement of a national screening of children in schools in the near future. I think this is going to be something you and your pediatrician will need to work out. I would definitely obtain a cholesterol screen on a child who had a family history of heart attacks before age fifty-five or a family history of high blood-cholesterol.

"The most important point I want to leave with you concerns developing good eating habits for your children. Educate them as you have been educated. Teach them what you have learned in the Save Your Life Cholesterol Plan. The eating habits they learn now could well carry over with them into adulthood and determine whether they become one of the coronary artery statistics."

"You covered it well." Evelyn stopped taking notes. "I am going to talk with our pediatrician. I would like to know our children's cholesterol level. I don't want them to be children whose parents are asymptomatic, yet they have a cholesterol problem."

"Good enough." Dr. Holly straightened her desk as Andy and Evelyn prepared to leave. "You have been great students. I know you are both going to be successful in your plan to develop healthy bodies. I encourage you to keep after it. Reach your full potential. Look great and feel tremendous.

"You should look forward to what Dr. Lowell Benjamin has to tell you. He will take you a step deeper into how to change your eating habits. You will find yourself changing your eating style after his visit."

6

THE SPECIFICS: WHAT DO YOU EAT?

D̲r. Lowell Benjamin is average height, in his fifties, has greying hair and a natural smile. He has kept in good physical shape, which gives him a demeanor of self-confidence and authority. He greeted the couple warmly as they entered his office.

"Good morning. I welcome you to the land of the free and fit. You are free to choose what you want to eat, and if we have anything to do with it, you will choose the Save Your Life Cholesterol Plan and become fit for the rest of your life."

"I like that," Andy said. "Actually, we have already chosen to carry through with this: if you will get us started with some specifics for each meal, we'll be well on our way."

"Do you have a list of menus?" Evelyn asked.

"No list of menus and no cookbooks," Dr. Benjamin began, "but I do go over enough of the specifics so you can adjust what you eat and what you cook accordingly. I want you to be able to cook for yourself, eat at someone else's home or at any restaurant you want, and still choose to eat properly. If you want a good reference cookbook, I recommend the American Heart Association's cookbook. It has some great recipes with a good low-cholesterol guideline to follow. However, we won't be that specific with you. We want to change your overall eating habits and let you pick your own recipes. What you are about to learn will allow you to make proper decisions on roughly 80 percent of what you will be eating. The rest you can find in the right cookbooks if you desire.

"Now, let's start with breakfast. What's your normal breakfast?" Dr. Benjamin looked at Andy.

"I'll tell you what it used to be: eggs, over light, several pieces of bacon, toast and butter with jelly, perhaps some orange juice, cup of coffee. That was the normal. Occasionally, when I ate at a certain restaurant in town, I'd get their 'All-American breakfast special,' which included biscuits and gravy, scrambled eggs with cheese, sausage, hash browns, and coffee. I always liked breakfast."

"Sounds like it." Dr. Benjamin was taking notes. "I'm sure you've already changed your habits for this meal a lot. I want to stress that breakfast habits are some of the easiest to change. There is usually no ritual associated with breakfast; usually rushed, the whole family sometimes doesn't eat together. So it's the most individualistic meal of the day. Breakfast food is easy enough to prepare for you to be very choosy without offending anyone."

"You're right," said Andy. "You don't hear of many husbands taking their wives out for breakfast by candlelight."

"True," responded Dr. Benjamin. "I'm going to take two approaches to breakfast. The first is that 90 percent of what you've been eating for breakfast is very high in cholesterol and saturated fat. Your breakfast has to change to some other type food."

"If cholesterol is your first topic," Evelyn said, "you won't get any argument from us on that. You can go on to topic number two if you like."

"Okay, topic number one: avoid cholesterol and saturated fat for breakfast; cut out the eggs, butter on your toast, bacon, ham, sausage, whole milk." Dr. Benjamin continued. "Now, I'm going to give you a replacement for your breakfast cholesterol. Topic number two deals with fiber, something we have not discussed with you. I'll tell you a little about fiber and then encourage you to switch from a cholesterol breakfast to a high-fiber breakfast."

"I don't think I'll like it, but go ahead." Andy had set his mind on a goal. "What exactly is fiber?"

"Fiber is a type of carbohydrate," Dr. Benjamin began his instructions. "The type I will be talking about is only found in plants. Most people understand what carbohydrates are, but I'll give you a simple review. Let's divide carbohydrates into individual chemical units that can stand by themselves or can join to make chains of units. The simplest carbohydrate unit, which stands alone or links with only a few units, makes up the sugars. The starches are made up when more of these simple units join together. The units in the more complex carbohydrates may number up into the hundreds. Of course, these sugars and starches can be easily digested by the body. Fiber resembles starches, but it can't be digested. It is simply bulk. There usually is a considerable amount of fiber in the complex carbohydrates.

"One good thing about eating fiber is that it is filling. Because it absorbs water, you can eat more foods with fiber and feel satisfied with fewer calories."

"What about breakfast?" Evelyn was trying to keep her notes in order.

"It's important to understand fiber before I say more about breakfast. Just hold your horses and I'll get there.

"I've been to Africa many times and worked in hospitals there. Medically speaking, I don't find three basic diseases related to the colon over there; yet a good deal of my practice in America is devoted to them. Carcinoma of the colon, diverticulitis, and appendicitis are all commonplace colon-related diseases in an American doctor's practice. I just don't see colon problems in these outlying African bush hospitals I visit from time to time."

"First of all, what is diverticulitis, and second, why don't they have those diseases in Africa?" Andy asked.

"Diverticulosis refers to the multiple pouches we find in most Americans' colons as they get older. These pouches resemble an inner tube pushing through the wall of a tire. When they become inflamed, you have an infected diverticulum, and that condition is called diverticulitis. Africans don't have the colon problems I mentioned because of their diet. Due to the bulk and fiber in their diet, they do not develop these pouches and thus no diverticulosis and no diverticulitis.

■ *Soluble fiber is good for lowering cholesterol.*
Insoluble fiber is good for your colon.

"Fiber is the name of the game that protects them. Their main food is casauva, a root filled with fiber that they pound into a meal. They add a little water to make sort of a dough, pile it as high as they can on a plate, then start making little balls about the size of a lemon, and dip them in a little sauce for taste. If you eat two meals a day of it, you have the highest fiber diet in the world. Not much nutrition, but high in fiber. Large stools, large stools every day, and no appendicitis and no colon cancer."

"Why would high-fiber diets keep you from having cancer?" Evelyn wanted to know.

"We're not really sure," Dr. Benjamin continued, "but it' thought that the fiber may move through the colon quickly an carry the materials that cause cancer with it, not leaving muc time for the cancer-producing materials to stay in contact wit the lining of the colon. But for whatever reason, fiber is impo tant for us to eat. And it's important for you to eat fiber for breakfast."

"Now you're back to the subject I want to know about," Evelyn smiled. "I can appreciate the emphasis on colon diseases. How does that fit into what I eat for breakfast?"

"It's the best way to keep your bowel movements regulated that I know of. A good high-fiber breakfast helps ensure a daily bowel movement.

"We recommend that you double or triple the fiber you now eat, and one of the best ways is by starting your day with a high-fiber breakfast."

"Okay, tell me what and I'll write it down." Andy picked up his pad once again.

"Begin with a fiber cereal and sprinkle some all-bran on the top. You'll hear later from another doctor about the importance of oat bran. In the meantime, get some oat bran cereal or make oat bran muffins. Add fruit and a couple of slices of whole wheat toast, and you'll already have over one-third of the total fiber you need for the day. The fruit is also an excellent fiber food."

"That would get mighty old every morning, wouldn't it?" Andy wasn't too keen on the prospect of this unappetizing food.

"I tell you, it's the easiest change you can make," Dr. Benjamin said reassuringly. "You can add variety, but make the fiber breakfast the basis to build on."

"Okay, what can I add for the variety part?"

"Pancakes, grapefruit, oatmeal, blueberry muffins, French toast, eggs—only the whites of course—waffles, pineapples, oranges, cantaloupe, cream of wheat, grits, strawberries, bananas, honeydew melon." Dr. Benjamin spouted off a quick list of many foods to go along with the basic bran breakfast. "Breakfast can range from fair to great, depending on what you eat and your attitude."

"You're right," Evelyn chimed in. "Fresh strawberries on a

bowl of 40% bran flakes, sprinkled with some all-bran, a fresh cup of coffee, wheat toast with jelly—served on the patio. Sounds good to me." Evelyn laughed and her husband nodded and smiled back.

"Okay," Andy agreed, "the patio part sold me. Basically, you want us to change from cholesterol to fiber for breakfast. I can handle that."

"It sounds really good to me," Evelyn said. "Dr. Benjamin, take us out to lunch. Figuratively speaking, that is."

"Of course, right this way to the basics for lunch," Dr. Benjamin started. "Try to hold back on meat and cheese. Eat some lunches that are entirely meatless. If you're going to eat a sandwich for lunch, stick with lower-fat meats such as chicken or turkey and avoid the meats higher in fats, which include most of the packaged lunch meat, hot dogs, and bologna. Start switching your protein from meat protein to vegetable protein. Bean soup is a good example of vegetable protein.

"You can get a salad at almost any restaurant in town. Just don't mess up the plan by pouring on the salad dressing. A good example of the effect of dressing was reported in a *Consumer Reports* article. It stated that the packet of Thousand Island dressing that comes with a McDonald's salad can give it more calories than a Big Mac has. Be aware of what dressing can do to a salad. Use a minimum of low-calorie dressing or spice it up with lemon juice.

"Baked potatoes have also become a common item on lunch menus. A baked potato with the skin and a good salad can be quite filling. Watch what you put on the potato, though. Use mushrooms and broccoli rather than butter or cheese."

"You make it sound pretty simple," Evelyn stated. "I can see how there's a base for lunch to start with, but we can experiment with what we want to eat and make changes from our base."

"Exactly," agreed Dr. Benjamin. "Just keep in mind what our

goal is—to cut cholesterol and saturated fat to a bare minimum, trim the fat, add complex carbohydrates to the point that they are making up the main part of your diet, even up to two-thirds of your caloric intake. And last, cut down on meat protein and replace it with vegetable protein."

"Do you want us to know what percent of our lunch should be complex carbohydrates, fat, and protein?" Evelyn asked.

"No, just the concept," Dr. Benjamin replied. "There is no way you can keep up with percentages, but you can make an intelligent choice every time you sit down to eat. Don't worry; before too long the right choices will become habits. Your lunch pattern will change to the right foods, and before you know it, you will no longer even desire the old standbys. The hamburger, fries, and milk shake plus a hot apple pie with ice cream for dessert will be replaced with a chicken sandwich with soup or salad without thinking twice."

"What are some other suggestions for lunches?" Andy liked variety and kept pushing for alternatives.

"Try tuna salad sandwiches, chili, vegetable soup, pea soup, burrito with refried beans, corn on the cob, pasta salads. Pasta bars are becoming more popular in fast-food chains. Wendy's has put in an excellent pasta bar for lunch or dinner. Pasta is a great alternative." Dr. Benjamin concluded his list to Andy. "It's the same principle—down on cholesterol, up on complex carbohydrates, and more of your protein from vegetables."

"Okay," Evelyn spoke up. "Now, what about dinner? You've made it pretty simple so far, but dinner is the main meal I have to come up with almost every evening. Can you simplify that, too?"

"Not as easily," Dr. Benjamin admitted. "You'll have to redo your recipes and look for new ones your particular family likes. Everyone's taste is different. If you understand the Save Your Life Cholesterol Plan, you'll be able to handle it well.

"We go by our rule of threes for guidelines. We want you to eat a minimum of *three pieces of fruit a day*. It's great to get this as snacks.

"We want you to eat *three cups of vegetables a day*. Whether you want to prepare your family three different vegetables or make them take three helpings of the same one is up to you. Of course, at least one serving of vegetables can be a salad or potato at lunch.

"As for beans, aim for *three cups a week*. There's lots of variety here with pinto, lima, kidney beans, chili—you get the picture.

■ There are <u>no</u> foods that contain "good" HDL-cholesterol.

"Now look at potatoes and grains: *three servings each meal*. We're talking cereals, baked potatoes, popcorn, rice, oatmeal, and a whole world of different types of breads and toasts. You can also count snacks of these foods toward the goal.

"And finally the meats."

"You're stuck on the number three so far." Andy chuckled. "You going to tell us to eat three bites of meat a day?"

"Not a bad idea, but we won't take it quite that far." Dr. Benjamin smiled. "We do keep to the rule of threes; aim for an average of *three ounces of meat a day*. Actually, four ounces is more realistic since that's about the least you can order in a restaurant or feel full on. The key is to remember to eat low-fat meat such as poultry or fish and shy away from the red meats, which are high in saturated fats and cholesterol. Also you need to include cheese and milk products in your daily total of meats. These items count as meat in our plan."

"You do have a way of simplifying problems," Evelyn said. "All I have to do is count to three, and I have my meal plan for the day. Now could you be a little more specific about what I can prepare for dinner?"

"Okay, write quickly," Dr. Benjamin began. "Try cooking chicken twenty different ways, all with the skin off, spaghetti, salads, broccoli, baked potatoes, scalloped potatoes, potato salad, French bread, corn on the cob, dinner rolls, roast turkey, green beans, lasagna with a little lean beef, stir-fried mushrooms and zucchini, whole wheat breads, baked corn, many types of fish, clams, oysters, lobster, and any number of vegetables."

"That's enough!" Evelyn quit trying to write it all down. "I get the point."

"She doesn't have that many different recipes to begin with," Andy interrupted. "That list will keep me full."

"The average American family utilizes fewer than twenty recipes repeatedly. So all you have to do is experiment and find which twenty new recipes your family likes.

"Keep an overall plan as you develop your new cooking and dieting habits." Dr. Benjamin prepared to give them a quick overall review. "Let me review what your goals ought to be.

"First of all, we want you simply to become knowledgeable on the facts about foods, what they will do for you, and what they will do to you. We want you to realize what you are eating whenever you eat an egg, red meat, cheese and other dairy products. You'll be surprised how much of these foods you eat every day. Just begin to acknowledge to yourself how much it is.

"Then, begin eliminating and substituting. Cut out the eggs. Remember, they're like poison. Don't add cheese to your sandwich. Find some low-cholesterol cheese at the market to cook with if you can't cut it out completely. Don't eat hunks of cheese for snacks.

"Change your breakfast habits. Some people can do this in a

single morning. Others have to ease into it. Whichever—do it. Begin to eat bran cereals as the mainstay of breakfast. Oat bran is preferable. Sprinkle 100 percent bran on whatever cereal you eat. Fix whole wheat toast, and put a little jelly on it for good taste. Add bananas or strawberries to your cereal."

"Just a minute, doctor," Andy interrupted. "I've heard about eating whole wheat or what's called whole grain bread for years. Why is whole grain bread so much better for us than regular processed white bread?"

"Good question," Dr. Benjamin replied. "I've told you about bran and how it's better for your digestive system, especially your colon."

"Yes, I remember."

"The outer coverings of grains provide fiber, which is the beneficial factor in the digestive process. Well, all this husk, or fiber material, has been removed from refined bread. Whole grain bread still has this roughage fiber and is therefore much better for your colon than refined bread."

"Is that why we can add a little jelly?" Andy asked. "Because that whole grain bread doesn't taste as good?"

"I wouldn't say that. Some people like it better. Many sandwiches are good made from whole grain rye or wheat bread.

"Now, let's get on with our review." Dr. Benjamin looked back at the outline he had just covered with the couple. "While we're on breakfast, let's cover milk. Whether you put it on your cereal or cook with it, switch to a low-fat milk. Two percent milk is no problem at all. The entire family will completely accept it within two weeks.

"When you select meat at the grocery store or restaurant, think fish or chicken. And instead of fried fish, think broiled or baked. Begin to eat meals without meat in them at all, or use it as a condiment on rice or the like rather than as the main food of the meal.

"Quit using butter altogether. Switch to margarine. Begin to fill up on potatoes, vegetables, beans, and pastas. Take larger and larger servings of these foods, and smaller amounts of the foods with fats."

"Dr. Benjamin," Evelyn put down her notes. "You haven't said much about between-meal snacks. That's one thing my husband and I will have the most difficult time giving up. Any good suggestions?"

"Sure. Find your favorites and stick to them. Spend a little extra money and buy that favorite fruit to keep in the refrigerator. Keep apples around. I'll tell you a favorite nighttime snack for me—that's popcorn and a diet drink. I like popcorn; of course, no butter. I could eat popcorn seven days a week. It's good fiber food, low in calories, and filling. That's what I mean. Find some snacks that you like and stick with them. Simply quit the Twinkies and Oreos and chips with dip and cheese and chocolate bars and the like, and snack on something good for you.

"You'll develop the same desire for your new snacks as you had for your old ones. I've realized that snacking is at least partly psychological. We need a break, and a good excuse for a break is a snack. What you eat is only a part of the desire. The fact that you get to stop what you're doing is almost equally important. Go ahead and take the break. Just adjust what you eat during that break.

"Okay. I think I've given you about all that I'm to cover. Go home and absorb what we've gone over and then come back for your appointment with Dr. Lamm about exercising and dieting. I think you'll find what he has to say the most interesting of all you've heard. He has the latest facts and figures from the medical literature about the effects of exercise on cholesterol and coronary heart disease. Just be ready to set some more goals.

"One reminder—almost every doctor in our plan has talked to you about the importance of motivation. I also want to encourage you to develop the right attitude toward all that you do, not just dieting. You can't have the right attitude toward dieting and exercising without an overall positive attitude about everything you do. This includes your work, your family, how you treat your friends and each other. We want you to reach your full potential in life.

"Different ones of us have stressed different aspects of how to improve your attitude. I like to stress motivational books. Invest in your library at home. Have the right books around the house for yourselves or your children to pick up and read. Spend time reading literature that stimulates your mind. Never start a trip without a book to read on the way, especially if you're traveling by air. Make good use of that time spent between flights in the airport. You can take charge of what you want to read on the plane; don't let the attendants decide for you. Have a good motivating book to read while you fly. You'll be surprised how much better you feel when you reach your destination. Even your image of yourself will be different if you make this one of your habits.

"With that, I'm going to leave you. I wish you both the best. I'm convinced you're on your way to success in your life-style of eating and your life-style in general."

Andy and Evelyn thanked Dr. Benjamin and left his office with the same enthusiasm they had when they decided to set their goals for dieting. They both were so much more knowledgeable about food and the physiology of their bodies. With this newfound knowledge, it would be much easier to eat properly. As a matter of fact, it would be difficult for them to eat the bad foods they had learned about. Their new eating habits will become a two-way street.

They were eager to find the role exercise has to play in their plan for becoming their best. They both knew how much better they felt when they exercised, but for weeks at a time they exercised very little, if at all. Then when they did get around to it, their bodies couldn't hold out well. They wanted to know the *whys* concerning exercise and their good health. They were fired up about their new images.

7

THE OAT BRAN-CHOLESTEROL RELATIONSHIP

When they came for the session on exercise, the Wilsons were instructed to drop by Dr. McClary's office first for some new information on foods that have received a considerable amount of publicity.

Dr. McClary pointed them toward two easy chairs in his comfortable office. He had been a Marine at one time, and this was reflected by the memorabilia all around his office. On the wall behind his desk hangs his patrol flag signed by all the men who served under him. Each survivor of the battle in which he was seriously wounded had autographed it.

He takes the Save Your Life Cholesterol Plan seriously. He has researched extensively the diet claims made about oat bran and niacin. He would be teaching the couple what he thinks is significant about these two subjects.

"There is one additional area to be covered before you complete your study of foods and start on exercise. I won't take long; I'll get right to the point. Taking less cholesterol and saturated fat into the body is one way of lowering your cholesterol count. The other side of the coin is getting rid of cholesterol in your body."

"You mean we can actually get rid of cholesterol that is already in our systems?" Evelyn inquired.

"Certain medicines and certain foods are known to lower your cholesterol count. The medicines, I won't go into; you will need your doctor's supervision if your cholesterol is high enough to be treated by drugs. And by the way, I feel you should be under your doctor's care if you cannot get your cholesterol below 200 on the Save Your Life Cholesterol Plan." Dr. McClary wanted to emphasize consulting a doctor if their cholesterol stayed high. "Not only that, but we want you to see your physician to have your cholesterol checked and recorded prior to beginning this program. Remember, your total cholesterol can be 200, but your HDL-cholesterol may be way out of line.

"You may have a normal total cholesterol and yet have a low HDL-C. An HDL-cholesterol below 35 is a risk factor for coronary heart disease, and your physician can advise you if it is too low. Remember our discussion concerning the ratio of HDL-C to total cholesterol. You may have a total cholesterol of 200, which you think is good. However, you may have a low HDL-C of 30. Your ratio would then be $200/30 = 6.66$, which is way over the 4.5 safe range. Just keep in mind the importance of your HDL-C in this cholesterol numbers game. We want to help you control your cholesterol through knowledge of what happens to the cholesterol you eat and manufacture in your bodies."

"You mentioned foods that can lower our cholesterol. What are they, and how much should we eat?" Andy was excited as he heard that something other than medicine could lower the cholesterol already in his system.

"We've mentioned fiber in your diet for bulk. We've talked about fiber cutting down on colon cancer, diverticulitis, and other related colon diseases. Well, I'm going to break that down a little more and explain how certain foods can lower your cholesterol. There are two types of fiber: water soluble and water insoluble. The water-insoluble types do have a significant positive effect on the colon as I just mentioned; but the insoluble ones do not have a significant effect on cholesterol." Dr. McClary was laying the foundation of what he wanted the couple to learn.

"What is an example of this insoluble type fiber?" Evelyn asked.

"Wheat bran is a very common one," Dr. McClary answered. "Many bran cereals are made from insoluble fiber and are very good for prevention of the colon disorders I've mentioned, but they do not have any significant effect on cholesterol. Only the water-soluble fibers do that."

"Okay, what about the water-soluble ones we're supposed to eat?" Andy persisted in his questioning.

"Thought you'd never ask," Dr. McClary quipped back. "We'll talk about two basic foods in this category: oat bran and beans. These two foods have been shown to lower blood-cholesterol. An article in the *American Journal of Cardiology* reports that a documented study from around the world suggests that eating a significant amount of such fibers helps protect you from coronary heart disease. This particular study used oatmeal, oat bran, or beans in its experiment. All of the patients tested had cholesterol levels above 260 mg/dl to begin with. They were fed 50 to 100 grams of dried beans or oat bran daily."

"Oatmeal, oat bran, or beans." Evelyn was writing this down as she spoke. "I can include that in my diet without much trouble. What's the difference in oat bran and oatmeal?"

"Oatmeal has oat bran in it," responded Dr. McClary. "Think of it being 60 to 70 percent as effective as oat bran itself."

"What effect did this water-soluble fiber food have on the patients you just mentioned in that study?" Evelyn continued.

"In less than two weeks their LDL-cholesterol fell, and their

HDL-cholesterol remained about the same. Thus, they improved their HDL/total cholesterol ratio significantly."

"How much did their cholesterol drop?" Evelyn was still writing.

"The report, along with another related study, showed the decrease to be in the 20 to 25 percent range, which is very significant. Since this report in the *American Journal of Cardiology* and another article with the same findings published in the *Journal of the American Medical Association*, we have incorporated oat bran, oatmeal, and beans into our diet program. We had been receiving occasional reports about the validity of such additions to the diet, but we were reluctant to recommend them officially until they were documented in these two accepted medical journals."

"What was the report in the *Journal of the American Medical Association?*" Andy asked.

"It was a study comparing the cost of two leading cholesterol-lowering drugs with oat bran," Dr. McClary explained. "You realized the significance of this study because it determined how much money it cost 'per year of life saved,' as they put it. Eating more oatmeal, oat bran, and beans can add some time on your life. The amount of oat bran used in the study was one and one-half cups per day. Basically, it showed that it's much less expensive to eat oat bran than to take the cholesterol-lowering medicines.

"I think the significant point made in that particular report was not that oat bran is less expensive and can lower cholesterol and decrease death from coronary artery disease. The report went one step further to show that for every coronary artery disease death averted, there were two and one-half heart attacks averted, and more than seven positive exercise tolerance tests averted. This means a patient could walk on a treadmill longer without developing chest pain." Dr. McClary looked at Andy to make sure the impact of this was sinking in.

"You lost me, doc," Andy interrupted. "What does that actually mean?"

"It means that we are talking about not only the quantity of life but also the quality of life. It means a simple thing like eating oat bran can result in a higher tolerance for exercise, fewer episodes of chest pain, fewer heart attacks, and even fewer coronary artery bypass surgeries according to this report. Plus, every heart attack averted means more income for that individual and less lost time from work with chest pain, heart attacks, and all the morbidity that goes with heart disease.

■ *Oat bran, oat meal, and beans may help protect you against coronary heart disease.*

"The conclusion was that for the public's overall approach to lowering cholesterol, dietary modification is preferred to a medically oriented campaign focused on drug therapy. Diet should be the first line of defense in the battle against cholesterol."

"How do oatmeal, oat bran, and beans work in lowering the cholesterol?" Evelyn was becoming very detailed in her notes.

"Right now, the way these water-soluble fibers actually work is under heavy investigation. We don't know exactly how they work, but several possibilities are being studied. Cholesterol is the main precursor of bile acids. Think of the chain of events going on in the liver and intestines as you try to understand the role of cholesterol and oat bran. Remember that the body gets cholesterol from two sources: the diet plus what is produced in the liver. Incidentally, this cholesterol accounts for the overall majority of the cholesterol in the body.

"Let's jump to the digestive system and tie it into this cholesterol cycle of events. Bile acids are needed to digest the food you eat. The bile acids, made from cholesterol by the liver, are passed from the liver by way of the bile duct into the intestines to emulsify the fat in foods to help facilitate absorption into the intestinal wall. The more bile acids are utilized, the more cholesterol is used up to make them.

"Now, how do oat bran and beans fit into the picture? It is thought that water-soluble fibers bind these bile acids, causing more to be excreted by the liver, thus using up more cholesterol.

"Another possibility of the way these water-soluble fibers work lies in the makeup of particles within the intestinal wall during the digestive absorption of food. This micellar formation is essential for cholesterol absorption from the intestines into the body. These water-soluble fibers found in oat bran and beans may interfere with this micellar formation within the intestines.

"One other possibility is that these water-soluble fibers may be acted upon in the intestines to form what is called short-chain fatty acids, which in turn could affect the actual production of cholesterol by the liver.

"For whatever reason, the water-soluble fibers found in oatmeal, oat bran, and beans have important cholesterol-lowering properties. That is why we recommend them in your diet."

"What you're saying," Andy interrupted, "is that these foods high in water-soluble fiber act like prescribed medicine in lowering cholesterol and are far less expensive."

"As I said before, we know it does work. The landmark report by the Lipid Research Clinics Coronary Primary Prevention Trial is the leading study that supports the importance of this relationship between cholesterol-lowering drugs and water-soluble fiber. The results of that report were based on known drugs that lowered cholesterol, and now we find these fiber foods can have a similar effect. Therefore, we can correlate what they reported concerning drug therapy with soluble fiber foods. Their ten-year trial demonstrated, in a group of patients who had extremely elevated cholesterol, a direct relation between consumption of a drug that lowers the cholesterol level and the actual reduction in their blood-cholesterol. The trial established the fact that there was a 2 percent reduction in the risk of having a heart attack or dying from a heart attack for every 1 percent reduction in total cholesterol level.

"That report on the excellent results of cholesterol-lowering medicine carries over directly to the *Journal of the American Medical Association*'s article that compared the cost of using the medicine versus oat bran. And you remember their conclusion. They prefer a broad public health approach to lowering cholesterol levels by changing diet rather than a medically oriented campaign focused on drug therapy.

"One thing to keep in mind is that the drugs are far more potent than water-soluble fiber. Some patients will have to take these prescribed drugs even if they are on a low-cholesterol diet and eating all the oat bran they can stuff in. The specific cholesterol-lowering medicines will continue to play a leading role in treating certain patients whose cholesterol remains uncontrollably high. But these patients will still need to remain on the Save Your Life Cholesterol Plan to ensure the best possible treatment of their problem."

"Is that why you emphasize being followed by a physician?" Andy looked at Dr. McClary for reassurance.

"Exactly right. For the majority of Americans, the Save Your Life Cholesterol Plan will suffice. But it may not do the job alone. Your private doctor has to take that responsibility."

"You're convincing me." Andy smiled. "How many beans and how much oatmeal or oat bran should we eat?"

"Before we get into *treating* elevated cholesterol, I'd like to get on the soapbox and preach you a little sermon, emphasizing what I've just said concerning your physician. The Save Your Life Cholesterol Plan is not meant to be a substitute for your doctor. We do not want you to treat yourself with this plan. I look at oatmeal, oat bran, beans, niacin, and cholesterol-lowering prescription drugs as treatment. I emphatically state that you should have your cholesterol checked by your physician, including your HDL-C as well as your total cholesterol.

"Use our plan as a guideline, but let your doctor decide if you should use niacin or one of the cholesterol-lowering prescription drugs. We will stick to encouraging you to develop an eating life-style that will lower your weight to normal, restrict your dietary fat and cholesterol, make oatmeal, oat bran, and beans a significant part of your diet, and develop an exercise program commensurate to your needs.

"With all that said, let's look at some of the specifics of eating these water-soluble fiber foods. Most of these studies used 50 to 100 grams of oat bran or beans per day."

"How much is that in cups or muffins?" Evelyn asked.

"It would be three to five muffins daily, but I don't expect you to eat five muffins a day, or even three every day for that matter. However, you can think of three muffins as being the equivalent of 50 grams of oat bran, and you strive for the amount daily. You get variety with oatmeal cereal for breakfast, bean soup for lunch, and a muffin with your dinner. Just use 50 grams as your goal every day. You can vary the beans; try navy, pinto, kidney, lima. And you can make great variations with oat bran muffins. Oat bran and beans have a similar effect gram for gram in their cholesterol-lowering property. One basic idea to remember is reported in the *Journal of the American Dietetic Association* article entitled 'Serum Lipid Response to Oat Product Intake with a Fat-Modified Diet.' This report suggests that the cholesterol level responds somewhat proportionally to the amount of water-soluble fiber eaten."

"So five muffins would be better than three?" Evelyn looked up from her notes.

"In one sense, yes," Dr. McClary responded. "But remember one thing. These studies were done on patients who had cholesterol levels over 165. A certain amount of these fiber foods may drop cholesterol 25 percent for these patients whereas someone with a more normal cholesterol level may not drop nearly so much. The point we're trying to make at the Save Your Life Cholesterol Plan is that developing certain eating habits will lower your cholesterol to a significantly low level and keep it there. Some programs emphasize only one aspect of this overall plan. We feel you should know everything that affects your cholesterol and develop your eating and exercise habits around this wisdom."

"So oat bran alone is not the panacea for cholesterol control?" Andy interjected.

"Absolutely not. Cholesterol is a very complex enemy, and the more weapons we have to combat it, the greater our chance of victory." Dr. McClary concluded his sermon on oat bran, putting it in its proper place relative to the overall fight against cholesterol.

"What about niacin?" Andy wasn't sure about this element he had heard the doctor mention. "What is it, and how does it work?"

Dr. McClary got up from his desk and began to pace slowly in front of the couple as he explained. "Niacin is another name for nicotinic acid, which goes by the brand names Nicobid and Nicolar. It's one of the B-complex vitamins.

"As far as what niacin can do in relation to your cholesterol, it is known to lower LDL-C and even to raise HDL-C. This is a recognized fact in the medical literature. Again, we don't know exactly how it works, but it seems to affect the liver's production primarily of VLDL-C and secondarily LDL-C, resulting in a decreased amount of these products in the bloodstream. What makes this such a good drug is its ability to actually raise the good HDL-C level in the body of many individuals."

"If niacin is so good, why isn't everybody taking it?" Andy wanted to know.

"That's a logical conclusion, but you have to look at the reports a little closer. Many of the studies reported in the *Ameri-*

can *Journal of Cardiology*, the *New England Journal of Medicine*, and the *Journal of the American Medical Association* used varying doses of niacin, many times large doses or they used niacin in conjunction with other cholesterol-lowering drugs. So, it's not a complete simple solution, but often a part of the solution. I feel niacin should be used at the discretion of your physician rather than my telling you to take a specified amount.

"Now, you have to ask what are the side effects of this drug. Niacin, especially if taken in a large dose at one time, tends to cause fairly severe flushing throughout the body. Patients complain of their ears turning beet-red and getting hot. Niacin can also cause intestinal disorders and dry skin. Some patients develop abnormal liver function studies. As a matter of fact, there have been reports of severe liver damage with some people taking niacin without being monitored by a physician!

"How would it be if I just started taking niacin in place of cutting down so heavily on all that good food with cholesterol?" Andy was wondering about being able to cheat just a little on his diet.

"No, for more reasons than one. First, the most important line of attack against cholesterol is diet. All of the medical journals are united on this. The best approach is to develop better eating habits and exclude fatty foods, cholesterol, and saturated fats. If you take some type of medication to do this for you, it will only hinder your developing the eating habits that are the only way to control your cholesterol for life. Second, even if you end up taking niacin or a prescription drug, the advice remains the same; diet is the first line of treatment of high blood-cholesterol.

"In that same light, I had a patient yesterday here in the office whose cholesterol was 286. She could not believe the report. She had been eating three oat bran muffins a day for the past three months. She said she had stuck to her low-fat cholesterol diet during this time, but when I asked her specific questions, she admitted to numerous breaks in her diet. She had not yet been on the Save Your Life Cholesterol Plan. She had been dieting as a martyr. It was a daily battle because she had not changed the eating habits in her mind. She had kept her old eating style right there in the back of her mind for quick referral.

"Some time ago, she had been placed on a diet simply to lower her cholesterol. She had been successful for about two months, and her cholesterol dropped from the 270 range down to 220. Then, she heard about oat bran muffins and started eating them, expecting her cholesterol to continue to drop. When she had her cholesterol checked again and it was higher, she came to me distraught because 'the oat bran didn't work.' She had been lulled into a trap. The oat bran had worked, but she had put too much faith in it and slacked up on her overall cholesterol and saturated fat intake. I now have her starting from scratch on the Save Your Life Cholesterol Plan. Hopefully, she will succeed in lowering her cholesterol to safe levels. I think she will be able to, but if not, she will have to use niacin and cholesterol-lowering drugs to supplement this plan."

"Would you mind summarizing your stand on the subject of oat bran and drugs in keeping our cholesterol down?" Evelyn requested.

"Sure, I'll be glad to give you a quick review before you go to your next doctor. First, we discussed certain products that can lower your cholesterol even after it is in your body. It has been known for quite some time that certain prescription drugs can do this. More recently, it has come to light that certain water-soluble fibers can have similar effects in lowering cholesterol; the main such fiber foods are oat bran and beans. These are common, everyday foods you can buy in a grocery store and feed to your family. No big deal, no doctor's prescriptions, no dangers, and relatively inexpensive compared to the cost of medications. We feel everyone should eat oat bran, oatmeal, and beans, daily if possible. The amount should be the equivalent of three to six oat bran muffins, 50 to 100 grams daily, supplemented with oatmeal cereal at breakfast and beans at lunch and/or dinner.

"We placed taking niacin in the same category as taking the known cholesterol-lowering drugs—under the care of a physician. We feel that if diet alone does not keep your total cholesterol in the 180 to 200 range, and your HDL-C and your total cholesterol are not safe, you need to be under the supervision of a physician. He or she should be following your cholesterol closely. This game called life is too important to play alone.

"Mainly, we want you to realize that cholesterol control is a complex matter. No one thing is going to make it happen. Exercise alone is not the answer, nor is eliminating certain foods while continuing to eat others rich in cholesterol. Neither is oat bran or niacin a panacea for cholesterol control. We want to stress the whole ballgame rather than just the winning touchdown. We want you to understand the entire picture of the cholesterol syndrome; the physiology of what happens when you eat cholesterol and that cholesterol enters the arteries in your heart. We want you to understand there are no symptoms of this disease. You may feel great, exercise daily, never know anything is happening in those arteries of your heart until the alarm is sounded by a heart attack. Your overall knowledge of cholesterol can act as the only warning system you may ever have. We want your minds. We want you to understand dieting so thoroughly that you will naturally avoid certain foods and naturally *want* to fine-tune the most important possession you own: your body."

Dr. McClary sent the couple on to their original destination at the session on the importance of exercise in relationship to cholesterol. Andy and Evelyn concluded this short session with a much better appreciation for what these doctors were trying to do for them. The couple realized they probably wouldn't eat six bran muffins a day for the rest of their lives

ut they would concentrate on eating more bran and having
ean soup more often on those cold winter nights. They would
ontinue to be acutely aware of fatty foods, cholesterol, and
aturated fats, avoiding the milk products and red meat and
oncentrating more on the carbohydrates, pasta, and baked po-
atoes. They have learned quite a list of things that have already
hanged their eating habits.

■ *High LDL-cholesterol = high risk of coronary
artery disease. High HDL-cholesterol = low risk
of coronary artery disease.*

This entire plan of dieting reminded them of the proverbial
:ory of the blind man feeling different parts of the elephant
nd describing what it must look like. When feeling the tail, he
escribed a long skinny animal; when feeling the trunk, he
escribed a tubular animal the shape of a huge snake; and
hen touching the legs, he described the huge beast it really
as. The couple realized the importance of being able to step
ack and see the whole, not just parts, of this beast called cho-
sterol. They were beginning to understand that all the parts
t together into one picture called the cholesterol syndrome
nd that the Save Your Life Cholesterol Plan could actually
lay a significant role in saving their lives for a healthy older
ze.

8

THE ROLE OF EXERCISE IN WEIGHT LOSS AND CHOLESTEROL CONTROL

Andy and Evelyn had heard how important the concept of exercise is in the Save Your Life Cholesterol Plan. They had also heard about new findings coming to light within the medical community concerning exercise and coronary heart disease. In recent years neither of them had exercised much; Evelyn tried aerobics for a few months and then lost interest. They both played tennis fairly frequently in the summer, but they became very sedentary during the winter months. However, they had set their goals, and nothing so far had stopped their efforts. They were not about to let exercise stand in the way of accomplishment.

They entered the office of Dr. Ed Lamm. It was obvious that he takes time out of his busy practice to exercise. He kept a small sports bag with his running clothes and shoes partially stuck behind a chair in the corner of the room. A tennis racquet was propped in the corner of the room just behind the coatrack, and behind his desk was a small picture of him at the finish line of some kind of foot race; he looked exhausted in the picture.

He certainly didn't look tired in real life. A clean-shaven man with a great tan and in casual dress, he looked great. He was comfortably informal as he motioned them to a seat in his office. He certainly fills the bill as the perpetrator of the exercise portion of the Save Your Life Cholesterol Plan.

"Good to see you two. Heard a lot of good things about you both. You look like you've trimmed down from the first description I heard."

"We're firming up a little, and we've lost a few pounds so far."

Andy had actually lost twelve pounds, mainly by cutting down on the amount of food as well as switching from 9-calorie fat to 4-calorie carbohydrate he had learned about earlier in the plan. He had not imbibed even an ounce of alcohol. Evelyn was four pounds down even though the program so far only hinted at how to really lose weight.

"It's surprising how you can lose weight simply by switching from a diet high in fat to one mainly of complex carbohydrates and vegetables and the like. By the time you get to the real weight-loss part of the plan, it will be a cinch." Dr. Lamm put them at ease with his reassuring words and compliments.

"What I am to go over with you is the importance of exercise along with your new eating habits. We are interested in your complete well-being, not just how you look. I don't know of anything that will make you feel in more complete control of your life than being in great shape."

"It's been a long time since I was in shape," said Andy. "I ran track in high school. I think that was the high point of my physical condition. Haven't really been in top condition since. You know, all that studying in college, and then working long hours after we married. My interests just haven't been centered on my physical condition. Encourage me and maybe I'll change my mind."

"I think you hit the nail on the head when you said your interests just haven't been centered on getting in shape," Dr. Lamm pointed out. "I think that's why most Americans are not in shape. It's because they choose not to be in shape. It's our own choice."

He looked at Evelyn. "You have chosen to be overweight. There was a time when I was overweight . . . by choice. I say by choice because never in my life have I ever accidentally eaten anything. Every bite I ever put in my mouth, I have chosen to put there—no accident.

"It's the same way with exercise. You either choose to exercise or choose to watch television or read a book or whatever else you choose to do. But you choose not to exercise. Exercise is unimportant to most people, and it's my job to make it very important to you. I'll show you that it is so imperative that you'll feel guilty if you don't exercise. Recent studies from the Centers for Disease Control in Atlanta imply that nearly 60 percent of adults in America do not exercise regularly. That's where the Save Your Life Cholesterol Plan fits in. You fall into that 60 percent."

"Dr. Lamm, I'm very active in my work. Don't you think I get enough exercise every day just in my work?" Andy considered himself a fairly active individual and didn't want to add an exercise program to his busy schedule. As a matter of fact, the tone of his comment was almost argumentative.

"Perhaps to some degree, but I want to stress the actual time you set aside for sustained activity. That's what stimulates your heart and your lungs as well as your muscles."

"How much time?" Evelyn inquired.

"It will vary for each individual, but in general, the more often, the better. I encourage you to spend a minimum of twenty to thirty minutes a day, five days a week. Most of us should try to exercise every day to some extent. Within a seven-day period, you ought to be able to exercise on five of them with some regularity. I want you to develop a habit of exercise. There will be times when you should rest your muscles, but don't look for days when you don't need to exercise.

"We use the same approach in this part of the program as in the eating portion. We want you to change your life-style by developing the habit of being active rather than sedentary. I would rather that you exercise lightly six days a week than to double up on two days just to get a certain amount for the week."

■ *The three main means of raising "good" HDL-cholesterol: (1) exercise, (2) cessation of smoking, and (3) control of obesity.*

"Then give us the facts." Andy settled down with pen and paper. "The most important thing so far in this Save Your Life Cholesterol Plan has been the factual information you have furnished. Once I know the facts, I feel nearly compelled to comply because I can almost see the physiology of what is going on in my body."

"Okay, we'll go with facts." Dr. Lamm sat down behind his desk and began to thumb through a stack of reprints from medical journals. "Most recent studies conclude that physically active individuals are at a lower risk for coronary heart disease than less active people, and no study in any of these articles reported a significantly greater risk of coronary heart disease for the more active individuals. I have over thirty-five articles here on my desk. I want to tell you what they conclude. When I add my own opinion, I'll tell you it's mine rather than someone else's. Fair enough on the facts?"

"Sounds fair to me," Evelyn said. "Start teaching."

"We will cover two aspects of exercise. The first will be from a dieting standpoint, and the second, the correlation of exercise and coronary heart disease.

"First, let me say that it's almost impossible to lose weight without exercising. I say *almost* because there may be one or two here or there who can lose without exercise, but I personally say to you emphatically—you can't lose weight without exercising." One thing appeared certain: Dr. Lamm was firm in his convictions.

"I'll tell you why exercise is so important. Remember way back at the first session, you were told in order to lose weight, you had to take less calories in and burn more calories off. Well, exercise is the burning-off of those calories, and many times the calories you utilize in exercise are the only difference between losing weight and maintaining weight."

"How many calories are we talking about here?" Andy still wasn't convinced in his own mind that exercise had to be an intricate part of his program.

"Later on, you'll get specific instructions on how many calories to shoot for every day, but let's say you find that you can maintain your weight by eating 1500 calories a day. You maintain that for two or three months on a strict diet, but it's a constant battle every day not to eat the amounts you would like to. You feel hungry all day, and sooner or later, you will run out of willpower and fall back to fulfilling your hunger desires. Let's say you find that you are completely satisfied by eating approximately 300 more calories a day. The exercise part of the program lets you eat that extra 300 calories. You'll end up feeling great because of your exercise and because you're maintaining your weight by burning off those extra 300 calories. Our plan aims at utilizing 300 calories a day through exercise, but for the time being, I want you to understand our concept of developing the habit of exercising. Develop the habit for a seven-day-a-week program with a five-day reality. Develop the life-style of exercise. You soon come to the realization that the winning edge lies in the habit of exercise. Exercise is something that only you can do for yourself alone. No one can do it for you, you can't inherit it, you can't buy it, and you can't substitute anything else for it. You will feel better than ever before."

"You're very convincing. I like your reasoning. You say exercise is essential to losing weight. What about after you get to your goal weight?" Andy's question was a little less abrasive. Something had just clicked in his mind to give him a new outlook on exercising—a positive mode.

"You asked the right question, but before I answer I want to encourage you not to let a sedentary life-style become an impediment to your overall health. There is a basic physiological answer to your question about whether you need to continue exercising *after* you have attained your goal weight, but there's a secondary aspect as well.

"Many factors come into play when we exercise. Certain substances are released in our bodies. Adrenalin is released; glycogen is broken down into glucose, making it available to be utilized by our muscles. The body calls on its reserves to gear up for peak performance. We don't understand all the changes that actually take place, but we know that exercise has more than just physiological effects; it does more than just build up muscle mass, improve the cardiorespiratory system, and possibly affect the bones in our body.

"There is also a mental aspect to exercising. Not only will you feel better physically, but you will also feel better mentally. This part of the exercise effect I don't understand, but I do know you develop a feeling of accomplishment, a feeling that you are in control of what you are doing, a good feeling about yourself, a feeling no one else can give you.

"In the article 'The Relation of Physical Activity and Exercise to Mental Health,' published in *Public Health Reports*, the author reviewed the claim that vigorous physical activity has positive effects on the mental health of individuals. Although more clinical trials must be made, some studies point toward the fact that exercise is an effective means of reducing anxiety and improving self-confidence. Also, similar findings appear in two major Canadian population surveys to support the significantly positive association between exercise and psychological well-being.

■ *The process of atherosclerosis in our coronary arteries begins in our teenage years or before.*

"In summary, you can find medical literature supporting the idea that physical activity and exercise are associated with reducing the symptoms of anxiety and with improving self-confidence and giving you a sense of well-being. But the proof of the pudding lies in your own experience with exercise. If you try an exercise routine for two months, I think you'll find that your attitude about yourself is consequently different from what it is now. You do develop some sense of well-being, of being on top of the situation, a sense of being in control. Regardless of what the reports show, I think you'll see a positive effect on your overall attitude, which in turn colors your whole life—your attitude toward your family, your work, and yourself."

Evelyn liked what she was hearing. She wanted to feel good about herself. For so long, she had suppressed the fact that she didn't really feel good about herself as long as she was overweight. She realized that once she began to diet and once she began to exercise, she could think of herself as a success. She agreed with what Dr. Lamm was saying and committed herself to whatever exercise program he would prescribe. In fact, she would look at exercise as a prescription.

"What about my question concerning exercise after you lose your extra weight?" Andy persisted in finding out if exercise will be necessary after he has achieved his goal weight.

"Okay, I'll give you the basic answer I promised. I assume you accept the fact that you must exercise in order to lose your excess weight. Now, I'm going to tell you the reasons you should continue to exercise, even after you have reached your goal weight.

"We have been basing our Save Your Life Cholesterol Plan for a healthier, longer life on protecting arteries in general and protecting the arteries in the heart in particular. We feel that since the number one killer of the American population is coronary heart disease, anything we can advise you to do that helps protect those arteries in your heart, the better off you'll be. Plus, once you develop a life-style that protects your heart, you won't have to work at it so hard. It will be something you habitually do without having to make such an effort to accomplish it."

Andy and Evelyn continued taking notes. They realized that Dr. Lamm's presentation was so straightforward, it was advice they would follow for the rest of their lives.

"We'll cover this part of the program in two parts. First, we'll review some articles that are specifically about exercise and our old friend HDL-C, high-density lipoprotein-cholesterol. Do you remember how important HDL-C is in relation to coronary heart disease?"

Andy thumbed back through his notebook. "Sure do. HDL-C is the good type of cholesterol. You want your HDL-C as high as you can get it; it's a protective agent that helps clear out the bad LDL-C. I know I want my HDL-C elevated as much as possible."

"Very good. I think you have the basics down pretty well. Now, let's look at what we believe is one of the most significant ways to increase your all-important HDL-C."

"You're going to say exercise. I can feel it coming. You're going to say that exercise can raise your HDL-C and that we should continue to exercise even after we lose our excess weight. Right?" Andy had read Dr. Lamm like a book. He knew the approach of these Save Your Life doctors.

Dr. Lamm laughed. "Right! To begin with, let's review some

of the specifics of LDL-C and HDL-C and then go on. Low-density lipoprotein-cholesterol is approximately 75 percent of total cholesterol in the blood. It is more specifically associated with coronary artery disease than is total cholesterol, which is the sum of all the cholesterol in the blood. LDL-C probably has a major role in transporting cholesterol from the blood to the cells of the body for use in routine metabolism. Evidence suggests that LDL-cholesterol causes the accumulation of cholesterol in the arterial wall, which may ultimately lead to the formation of what's called atherosclerotic plaques—known as hardening of the arteries.

"Now for the high-density lipoprotein-cholesterol. HDL-C, as we are calling it, has been found to be four times greater than LDL-C and eight times greater than total blood-cholesterol in predicting the development of coronary atherosclerosis. In the medical journal *Circulation*, it was pointed out that for each 10 mg/dl change in HDL-C concentration in the blood, there was a 50 percent alteration in cardiovascular risk. This study dealt with patients who had very high cholesterol in their bloodstream, much higher than the general population, but the importance of HDL-C in protecting one's coronary arteries holds for all."

Evelyn looked up from her notes. "Now, just tell us how to raise our HDL-C."

"Very good request. We'll go with the premise suggested by investigators that HDL-C has an antiatherogenic effect on arteries and that we should do all we can to increase HDL-cholesterol levels.

"It was first noted that in comparing athletes who performed endurance sports with individuals who were sedentary, the HDL-C concentration in the blood of the athletes was statistically significantly higher. Studies were then begun to see if there was any close relationship between how much one exercised and how much one's HDL-C increased. Such studies suggested there was indeed a close response of exercise and

HDL-C, and they showed that HDL-C levels of individuals increased proportionately with the miles run per week. So, I encourage you to exercise, and the more you exercise, the better. You will be your own judge of the amount you do. I will only give you guidelines, but strive for an habitual *daily* exercise program, which will total the equivalent of fifteen miles of running or walking per week.

"I am not certain what long-distance running will do to your joints, especially your knees. We don't advocate marathon running. We are advocating a systematic progression in your exercise until you reach specific goals in relation to your oxygen needs as determined from your heart rate. More on that later. Right now, let's continue with our reports.

"I found an interesting report from the publishers of the *New England Journal of Medicine*. They reviewed forty-seven studies of the suggestion that physical activity helps prevent coronary heart disease. Sixty-eight percent of these studies showed a statistically significant inverse association between physical activity and coronary heart disease. The more you exercise, the less coronary heart disease seen.

"This is related to information coming out of the Centers for Disease Control in Atlanta in a recently published article entitled 'Physical Activity and the Incidence of Coronary Heart Disease.' This study goes further than any I've seen in stressing the importance of exercise in preventing coronary heart disease. It reported that existing medical literature does indeed support the direct correlation between physical activity and coronary heart disease; the person who exercises stands a lesser chance of a heart attack than one who doesn't exercise. This has been consistently observed in the literature of well-designed studies.

"I think this report from such a knowledgeable and accepted medical authority as the Centers for Disease Control is one of the most significant reports of the last decade concerning the importance of exercise in combating coronary heart disease in America. I cannot stress the importance of their findings too much.

"You remember the three factors that physicians say are the leading causes of coronary heart disease?" Dr. Lamm looked at Andy.

"Sure, one of the first doctors we saw told us that: high blood pressure, high cholesterol, and smoking."

"Okay. Let's take those three factors and see how they relate to each other.

■ *EXERCISE is a major factor in prevention of coronary artery disease.*

"We all know that coronary heart disease is our biggest enemy as far as our health is concerned; bigger than cancer of the breast, cancer of the lung, cancer of the colon, cancer of the uterus, cancer of the ovaries. Simply stated, the blockage of the arteries of our hearts by cholesterol is responsible for more deaths yearly than all forms of cancer combined. We are well aware of the severity of cancer because the American Cancer Society speaks and we all listen. Well, the problem of cholesterol and coronary heart disease is worse than all the cancer the American Cancer Society tells us about. We at the Save Your Life Cholesterol Plan want to speak and be heard in the same way.

"That is why some proponents of this plan are calling it the most important singular plan to improve the overall health of the American citizen. We realize that if we can educate the American people on diet and exercise, we have a far greater potential to save many more lives than we could by treating diseases after the fact.

"So let's see how we can best beat this disease. Let's go after the most important factors, the three you just mentioned, and see how they compare. Then, see how those three established culprits relate to the effect of exercise on coronary heart disease.

"This report from the Centers for Disease Control first shows these three factors in relationship to each other. It shows a risk ratio for each of the three. Let's see how each factor stands as far as risk for developing coronary heart disease is concerned. First, look at high blood pressure. If a person with a systolic pressure, the first number in the blood pressure reading, higher than 150 is compared to a person with a systolic pressure less than 120, the risk factor for developing coronary heart disease would be 2.1. This means that the person with the higher blood pressure would have more than twice the probability of developing coronary heart disease than the individual with the lower blood pressure.

"Now, look at the risk factor for an individual having a cholesterol reading greater than 268 and one with a cholesterol reading less than 218. In that case, the individual with the higher cholesterol has a risk factor of having coronary heart disease 2.4 times greater than the person with the lower cholesterol reading.

"Last, compare the smoker who smokes a pack a day or more with someone who doesn't smoke at all, and that risk factor is 2.5. The smoker has a two and one-half times greater chance of developing coronary heart disease than the nonsmoker."

Dr. Lamm pointed toward a comparative chart of the factors he just presented:

Risk Factor	Risk Ratio for Developing Coronary Heart Disease
High blood pressure	2.10
Elevated cholesterol	2.40
Smoking	2.50

"Now, do you understand the importance of these risk factor comparisons between smokers and nonsmokers, hypertensives and normotensives, and individuals with elevated cholesterol and lower cholesterol?"

"Yes," responded Evelyn. "All three factors more than double your chances of having coronary heart disease. All three, I'm going to avoid like the plague."

"I understand completely what you're saying about the accepted factors that increase our risk of having coronary heart disease," Andy said. "Now tell us how all this relates to exercise."

"I'll answer that question and, at the same time, answer your question about not exercising after you've lost your excess weight." He looked at Andy and hoped he realized the importance of accepting the facts of these studies.

"Try to think of not exercising as a disease—a disease you alone can cure, a disease you don't have to go to the doctor for. I want you to look at not exercising in the same way you look at actively smoking. I want you to see it as being that important. I want you to see it in the same way as high blood pressure and high cholesterol in your blood. I want you to view exercise as a medicine you can take to help prevent coronary heart disease as you get older. I want you to understand all the ramifications of exercise as related to diet and cholesterol.

"The reason I want you to visualize exercise as being so important is based primarily on this study we've been discussing. It shows the risk factor of developing coronary heart disease is markedly increased for individuals who do not exercise. As a matter of fact, when individuals who were sedentary were compared with those who exercised, the sedentary group's risk factor of developing coronary heart disease was a whopping 1.9 times greater than the group that exercised. Let that sink in. Neither of you would think of smoking because you understand how bad that is for your health. Well, we have just put not exercising in the same ball park as smoking. Compare that risk factor of 1.9 for not exercising with the risk factors for the three leading causes of coronary heart disease just mentioned. We can see that smoking, high cholesterol, and high blood pressure have relative risks only slightly greater than inactivity."

"From my notes, it looks like a sedentary life-style has a risk factor of 1.9, compared to 2.1 for high blood pressure, 2.4 for elevated cholesterol, and 2.5 for smoking." Andy really was taking this report seriously. "So I need to look at not exercising as a significant risk factor for my having coronary heart disease?"

"Correct. I think such reports at least suggest that exercise on a regular basis should be stressed as vigorously as the other three risk areas. I believe exercise is that important, and I encourage you to exercise just as much as the other doctors have encouraged you to cut your cholesterol. Let's look at that chart of risk factors in the proper relationship."

Risk Factor	Risk Ratio for Developing Coronary Heart Disease
Smoking	2.50
Elevated cholesterol	2.40
High blood pressure	2.10
Sedentary life	1.90

"That is extremely interesting," Andy responded. "I have a friend who is big on exercising, and I've always thought he was some kind of a nut. Now, I'm going to have to change my opinion of him. Do you have any more medical literature related to exercising or not exercising in conjunction with heart attacks?"

"Yes, as a matter of fact, there are some very interesting ones. Way back in 1953, a study in *Lancet*, a British medical journal, reported that conductors on those double-decker buses in London had only 46 percent the mortality from coronary heart disease when compared to their cohort bus drivers the same age. Of course, the conductors were running up and down stairs all day while the drivers just sat all day. The same journal also reported similar findings for postal delivery workers who walked their routes every day as compared with the postal clerks who worked inside with much less activity.

"Also, in a study of 16,936 male Harvard graduates, men who were sedentary had a 64 percent higher risk for a first myocardial infarction than did their classmates who exercised a minimum specific amount each week.

"I think vigorous physical exercise plays a very significant role in reducing the incidence of coronary heart disease. I'm sold on the idea and hope to sell you on it, too."

■ *You can exercise daily and still have a heart attack from high blood cholesterol.*
KNOW YOUR CHOLESTEROL LEVEL.

"Doc, you've sold me. I'll set up some type of exercise program. And I think my wife will join me. How much are you suggesting we exercise?" Andy had resigned himself to developing some type of exercise program.

"First of all, I want to tell you both there is no set formula for relating exercise to HDL-C. Even in the medical literature there is some disparity between reports concerning the optimum exercise. We do know that exercising will elevate the protective HDL-C and that the higher the HDL-C, the better. Remember, the HDL-C has been found to be four times greater than LDL-C and eight times greater than total cholesterol reading in predicting the development of coronary atherosclerosis. As much as I would like to tell you that if you run x number of miles a week for ten weeks, your HDL-C would go up x points, that simply is not the case. We have to speak in relatives, in probabilities, in trends. However, the basis in fact is definite. It has been tested. We know exercise is beneficial, but we can't talk specific amounts of exercise for each of you as individuals.

"In two articles, one from the *Journal of the American Medical Association* and the other from the *New England Journal of Medicine*, we find that long-distance runners had HDL-C levels significantly higher than a control group of nonrunners. And similarly, when three groups were compared, the sedentary control group had a low HDL-C, while joggers had a significantly higher level, and marathon runners had even higher levels.

"These reports, as well as others, point out what appears to be a direct relationship between the amount of exercise and the magnitude of the HDL-C increase.

"We'll look first at reports on the effects of mild physical exercise on HDL-C. One such article published recently in the *British Medical Journal* suggested that even mild regular physical exercise would cause a significant elevation in HDL-C."

"What do they consider mild exercise?" Andy inquired. "I think that's the kind I would go for."

"In that particular study, the subjects walked and jogged for nine to fifteen miles each week. That's an example of why it is so difficult to pinpoint exact amounts in so many of these studies; you know the ones who ran fifteen miles surely exercised more than the individuals who walked nine miles in the same period of time. I simply want you to look at it proportionally—the more you exercise, the greater the tendency to increase your HDL-C.

"An article in the *American Journal of Cardiology* is a little better as far as spelling out the particular exercise. That report showed a good response in elevating HDL-C on an exercise program that lasted three weeks. The exercise consisted of activities that induced up to 80 percent of the maximal heart rate during three twenty-minute periods daily for five days a week. Their exercise consisted of a mixture of jogging, short sprints, calisthenics, swimming, cycling, and brisk walking. I'll describe just what is meant by maximal heart rate shortly.

"Similar results were reported in the medical journal *Circu lation* for patients who exercised at 70 percent of maximal oxygen uptake three times a week for twenty to forty minutes over a three-month period."

"I'm getting the point of what you're saying." Evelyn looked at Dr. Lamm as she put her pen down for a rest. "You are saying that exercise will indeed raise our HDL-C, and that we should exercise even after we have lost our excess weight to help in that HDL-C/total cholesterol ratio we heard about before."

"Exactly. Very well taken. Don't let achieving your goal weight circumvent your overall health plan. Keep exercising."

"You mentioned something I would like explained. You said that the exercise consisted of 70 percent maximal oxygen intake. What does that mean? You also said the exercise in another report induced a heart rate up to 80 percent of maximum. What does all that mean?"

"It gets pretty detailed," Dr. Lamm replied, "but it is a good point of discussion. Let me try to simplify the physiology of our bodies during exercise. Basically, two things happen. One, the muscle exercising begins to require more oxygen, and two, the heart begins to pump out more oxygen containing blood to the exercising muscles. This increase in cardiac output in sustained exercise is about four times its resting output, and it is the result mainly of an increase in heart rate. There is a direct correlation: the greater the exercise, the greater the need for oxygen by our muscles that are exercising, the greater the need for oxygen in the blood to be pumped quickly to those muscles, and the greater the increase in heart rate."

"So knowing the amount of increase in heart rate becomes important in knowing if we're exercising enough?" Andy asked.

"That's right. But let's look at why it's important. The very best measurement of the effect of an exercise and of physical fitness is called VO2 Max. This represents the oxygen consumption of the muscle tissue. In other words, the amount of oxygen consumed relates directly to the amount of work the muscle does when it exercises. The more the muscle exercises, the more oxygen it will need and consume. If we could measure this oxygen uptake, we could be fairly exact about how much you are really exercising."

"Is it difficult to measure the amount of oxygen taken up by our muscles?" Evelyn asked.

"Yes, it is," Dr. Lamm responded. "But since there is a direct correlation between the amount of oxygen used by the muscle and how fast the heart beats to get it there, we simply measure your heart rate to ensure that the exercise you're doing is enough to get the response we want. Heart rate is not as exact as VO2 Max, but it gives us a pretty good indication if your muscles are exercising enough to make the heart pump that extra oxygen to them quicker. If the heart is pumping quicker, the heart muscles are improving with each heart beat."

Andy interrupted. "Let me see if I have this right. The more you exercise, the more oxygen your muscles need, and the heart responds to this need by beating faster to deliver the extra oxygen to the muscle."

"That's exactly right. In healthy people, the relationship between heart rate and oxygen uptake by the muscles is nearly a direct ratio.

"Now, to make all this practical. Let's see what it takes to develop optimal fitness for you as an individual."

"Should we strive for this optimal fitness you're talking about?" Evelyn inquired.

"I thought you'd never get to this point in your thinking. I want you not only to strive for this optimal fitness; I want you to set as your goal that a year from today, you are going to be in the best physical shape you have been since high school. It will surprise you how close to that high-school physical condition you can come. I want you to be able to evaluate your exercise. You can judge whatever exercise you're doing to see if it is physical enough by simply counting your pulse. I want you to exercise at least five times a week, and each session should last twenty to sixty minutes of exercise that is vigorous enough to get your heart rate between 60 and 80 percent maximum. I want you to keep the rate at that percent maximum continuously throughout each exercise period.

"What exercises you do, I will leave up to you. Develop in your own mind a sense of how good your exercise is. Learn what your heart rate is doing with each type of exercise. Then, you will realize that playing golf is no comparison to playing a tennis match, and that playing doubles in tennis doesn't compare to running three miles. You will need to develop your own exercise program to fit your physical needs. I want you to start slow and build gradually to your peak physical performance and then work to maintain that peak."

■ COMMIT TO EXERCISE.

"So, if I'm to exercise enough to get my heart rate up to between 60 and 80 percent of maximum, how do I know my maximum heart rate to begin with?" Andy asked.

"As a rule of thumb, your maximal heart rate can be estimated by subtracting your age from 220. All you have to do then is take 60 to 80 percent of that figure to see if your exercise is vigorous enough."

Dr. Lamm pointed to a chart on his desk for easy reference.

220 − age = maximum heart rate

$$\underline{\times \text{ percent of maximum exercise desired}} = \begin{array}{l}\text{goal heart rate} \\ \text{for duration of} \\ \text{exercise period}\end{array}$$

"Okay, I'm forty-two years old." Andy started figuring. "And 220 minus 42 equals 178. I will use 80 percent as my goal. Eighty percent of 178 equals 142. So you're instructing me to strive for an exercise program that will sustain my heart rate in the 140 range while I'm exercising. That's a very rigorous exercise, but I'll use that as my goal."

"Sure, it will be tough—but worth it. As you can see, we're talking about really working your body. We want you to take this program seriously. We want you to look at your body as the most important investment you have in life, to encourage you to protect your investment to the max. Most people would feed and exercise a million-dollar racehorse better than they take care of their own bodies. You must look at yourself as much more valuable than any racehorse."

"You've sold me. How much do you suggest we exercise?" Again Andy wanted the specifics to follow through.

"It will vary, of course. If you're losing weight, you should exercise almost daily. If you are sustaining your weight, use the same habit goal but with thirty minutes a day five times a week as a bare minimum. Remember, the idea is simply to develop the habit of exercising regularly. You will be much more successful if you plan for time each day of your life for your workout."

"What do you consider vigorous?"

"Exercise where you know you've had a workout. You need to get your heart rate up to 140 and keep it there. That means you will be breathing hard. You may be able to talk, but it will be an effort. That means if you include walking, you are going to have to go at it as if you were trying to break the first four-minute mile. A stroll won't do it. Jogging is one of the easiest exercises for time and distance consistency. Swimming can do, but it has to be constant without frequent rest periods, which will let your heart rate drop.

"Remember, it may take months before you reach your peak. It needs to be gradual. Set a comfortable pace and work at increasing it daily until you reach your goal. There are many different types of exercises you can choose from, but you should know how they're rated and how long you should spend doing each one."

"Would you give us a list of exercises with their intensities?" Evelyn asked.

"So you want a list of exercises to do? Okay, I'll give you generalities and then some specifics. Just remember, using 300 calories a day by exercising is usually the difference between losing weight and holding your own. It is also the difference between being able to eat the volume most people want and still maintaining weight at the stated goal. I want you to pick exercises that utilize at least 300 calories per session. You will be surprised at how much food you can eat once you have lost your excess weight and begin the maintenance part of the program. By exercising off 300 calories and eating the foods advised in the Save Your Life Cholesterol Plan, you will never have that sense of hunger, the feeling that you're not getting enough to eat—ever. And you will have developed different eating habits. You will feel full."

"So, our goal will be to use 300 calories a day in exercising?" Andy began to take notes again.

"Three hundred calories a day. I'll give you a good basic rule as a benchmark for all your exercises. Think of one mile as 100 calories, whether walking or running. Actually, walking is about 10 percent less, but we won't get that precise. Think of walking three miles or jogging three miles as the benchmark and relate other activities to that. The figures I'll be giving you will be related to calories expended. The amount of work you do to expend them depends on the figure for your 60 to 80 percent maximal heart rate. But remember, I'm talking about brisk walking, walking like you have to catch a plane you're about to miss. Walking a mile burns as many calories as running a mile; it just takes longer.

"One additional comment on your maximum heart rate. If you are just beginning an exercise program, the percentage of maximum heart rate to shoot for should be toward the 60 percent of the range. If you are beginning to exercise, the 60 to 75 percent range will strengthen your cardiorespiratory system and at the same time allow you to burn fat. As your physical condition improves, you can gradually increase toward the 80 to 85 percent figure, which is the percentage for the very well-conditioned individual.

"Personally, I consider myself in good physical condition. I am 47 years old; subtract that from 220 and I have 173 as my maximum heart rate. When I jog three miles, my heart rate holds between 130 and 138 beats per minute. That means I am at 75 to 80 percent of my maximum heart rate. I am running fairly hard to do that and don't think I will progress much beyond that rate. However, I utilize my 300 calories and keep my heart fit while I'm doing it. Just remember, in my case, I am sustaining this heart rate for twenty to thirty minutes to utilize 300 calories.

"I want each of you to develop your own exercise program. Each program will probably be different, but try to do some part of your programs together. I firmly believe that it helps a marriage if the husband and wife exercise together. Even if it's only a drive to the track to jog at the same time. They may not jog at the same pace, but at least they're at the track together. I've also seen a husband and wife always go their separate ways to exercise and end up spending time exercising that should be spent together. We want you to be your best, and that includes a good marriage. Exercise together whenever possible.

"As you work on developing what suits your style for exercise, I have some suggestions. Set your program up wisely to fit what you like to do. Studies show that about 50 percent of the people who begin an exercise program quit after a period of time except for the walking programs where the persistence rate is nearer 75 percent. So, keep it simple and interesting. Walking can be a good base to work from. I would advise mixing the exercises to keep them as interesting as possible. Set specific goals for how long each session will be, how many sessions a week you will do, and then persist.

"I am going to make estimates from a number of sources, giving you some averages and comparisons to which you can relate your own exercise. These numbers are relative as far as you are concerned. Calorie-burning is not that exact from one individual to another, but it will give you some indication of which exercise you can do and how long you should do it.

"Remember that one mile of walking or running nets you 100 calories burned. A thirty-minute walk will net you approximately 150 calories. So if you are going to rely on walking alone to reach your goal of 300 calories, you will need to persist for an hour. With running, simply time yourself during an average mile run. Most joggers can run an eleven-to-twelve-minute mile. At that rate for thirty minutes, you have your 300 calories. As you begin to get into good shape, you can get fairly consistent with thirty minutes of running and can utilize up to 450 calories in a single thirty-minute session.

■ *Exercise goal: 300 calories per day (1 mile walking/jogging burns 100 calories).*

"Exercising on a rowing machine for thirty minutes puts you in the 150-calorie category. Swimming is about equal to that. Bicycling is in the 200-calorie-per-thirty-minute category. Tennis is also in the 200-calorie range. Aerobic dancing fits in this thirty-minute range also.

"If you are looking for those exercises that burn up the most calories, look at the indoor court exercises. Racquetball, handball, and squash are excellent for the 300-calorie thirty-minute range, especially when you frequently play an hour or more of sustained effort in these sports. Cross-country skiing is also in the same 300-calorie thirty-minute range group.

"Finally, near the top of the list is stationary bicycling, which is in the 450-calorie thirty-minute range if sustained at the twenty-mile-per-hour work load.

"Pick out the exercises you enjoy most. Mix them up and make exercising an enjoyable occasion. There are lots of ways you can utilize your time exercising for other things. You can place your exercise bicycle or jogger or rowing machine in front of your television so you can watch the news while exercising. You can listen to tapes while you walk or jog—anything from music to sermons to self-help tapes. There is no need to look at your exercise time as wasted time if you feel you don't have the time to spend on exercise alone.

"Again, I want to encourage you to make exercising a family affair every chance you can. I suggest you go to the track to walk or jog together. I encourage you to buy an inexpensive stopwatch to time yourself in your walking and running. Buy yourself some good jogging shoes, shorts, and thick cotton socks to exercise in. Invest in yourself. Get serious about getting your body fit."

"How much exercise do you suggest we do once we get our weight off?" Andy persisted in his need for specifics.

"As you recall, I alluded to a pretty good correlation between the HDL-C elevation and amount of exercise performed, so I will say that a five-to-seven-day-a-week program is generally ideal even after you have stablized your weight. However, most studies in the medical literature report a significant effect with as little as thirty minutes a day three days a week. As I mentioned earlier, I recommend striving for a daily exercise program, which in reality turns into a five-day-a-week situation.

"Also, I encourage you to rest your muscles every second or third day. By that I mean you can ease up on the intensity of your exercise intermittently. Whatever you do, don't push on when your body is telling you to rest. Each individual will be different, but I want you to develop a pattern of exercising. I like to try to exercise some every day because of the life-style effect it has. If you plan to do some form of exercise every day, you will soon develop that pattern as a life-style. Then if something comes up that prevents you from reaching that goal one day, there is no great loss."

"Okay," Andy agreed. "I will plan to exercise at least five times a week for at least thirty minutes each session. I think I'm way too heavy to jog, so what do you suggest I start my program with?"

"You look determined to me. Start walking today. Since you need to lose weight, see what pace it takes to begin to increase your heart rate. You may feel fatigued after ten minutes of walking the first day. Then walk only ten minutes. But the next day, try twelve. Continue until you're at thirty to forty minutes at a good pace. Each day, increase the length and briskness of your walk. Count your pulse when you finish and use that as a gauge of how you're doing. The experts use oxygen consumption formulas, but as I've said, that correlates fairly well to heart rate. You'll be able to tell when you are really exerting yourself.

"After approximately one month, I want you to start mixing jogging with your walking until you are half walking and half jogging. Your eventual goal will be to jog the entire period of thirty minutes. Set your goal for the 300-calorie mark, whether walking an hour or jogging one-half hour. Begin with continuous exercise on a daily basis. It needs to be continuous rather than start and stop. Then you can gradually build up the intensity of the exercise. The duration should gradually increase also, but I like for you to be fairly consistent on duration and vary the intensity. One point I want you to remember: if you go several days without exercising, simply start again on your plan. You don't want to exacerbate an already serious health problem by returning to your old nonexercising habits."

"What about me?" Evelyn asked.

"Review the list of exercises we just mentioned and pick out what you want to do. Basically, the best way to burn calories is to do exercises that use large muscle groups of both arms and legs for the entire period of time. That's why continuous activities like jogging, swimming, walking, and cycling are such good forms of exercise. We need to find you a combination of exercises that use large muscle groups. What sports are you interested in?"

"I like tennis. And some of us have signed up for racquetball lessons. I like that sport. I also took golf lessons one summer, but don't have the time to play consistently."

"Okay, let's go from there. Golf shouldn't even be counted in the exercise program if you ride in a cart. Play golf if you like but play it for a sport only. As far as expending calories, your racquetball game is about twice as good as tennis. Plan your jogging program with a mixture of tennis and racquetball and progress in intensity in all three areas. Build your jogging up to the point that you really put some exertion on your heart and lungs. Intersperse some sprinting with your jogging.

■ *Exercise decreases the risk of coronary heart disease.*

"As far as your tennis, you can't count playing doubles. There is too much resting time in doubles. That will fall in the same category as golf. I like to keep the breaks between points and matches to a minimum in order to make the exercise as continuous as possible.

"One other thing I need to throw in here is the fact that you should have a five-to-ten-minute warmup before and after exercising to stretch your muscles. Touch your toes for a count of ten several times; then cross your feet and touch your toes for counts of ten. Take a giant stride with your left leg and hold it as you stretch out your leg muscles; then do the same with your right. Place one leg on a rail about waist high and stretch out and touch the toes of the elevated foot. Then the other leg. You want all your muscle bundles slowly stretched to maximum length before you start your exercise. You also need to repeat these stretching maneuvers after your exercising.

"Just remember, I want you to exercise in such a fashion that you keep your heart rate at a sustained elevation."

"So you're stressing continuity in whatever exercise I do. Just to keep my heart rate up?"

"Exactly. However, you need to get into the habit of doing short exercises during the day. For example, quit using the elevator and begin utilizing the steps. Even eight or ten flights of stairs will give your heart a little push. Also, any breaks you have during the day, don't sit down and sip a cup of coffee; instead, take off for a fifteen-minute walk. Stay active. If you eat lunch near your office, walk to lunch instead of taking a taxi or driving. Spend more time moving those muscle masses in your legs and arms.

"I want to finish by encouraging you to work on your goals and to work on your attitudes. One thing I want to stress concerns your motivation. You can't read enough books, you can't listen to enough tapes, you can't attend enough seminars to stay motivated properly. You don't just become motivated one day and that's it for the rest of your life. It's similar to taking a bath; you need to do it every day."

Andy and Evelyn felt almost exhausted as they looked up from the yellow legal pads they had been taking notes on. Dr. Lamm had succeeded in stimulating each of them to realize the importance of exercise not only in losing weight, but in sustaining good health as well. Their lives were slowly changing for the better. They were seeing themselves in a different light. For the first time in their lives, they understood the importance of good physical health. They realized it's not something you can go to a store and buy, no matter how much money you have. They have learned something worth far more than the money they had paid to learn about the Save Your Life Cholesterol Plan. After years of infatuation with quick weight-loss diets, they were ready to face reality concerning the relationship of diet and overall health. Dieting is so much more than losing weight; it is a way of life.

They were now ready to attend their last session of the Save Your Life Cholesterol Plan on the process for losing weight. This session was the main reason Andy had become interested in the program. Yet it seemed almost anticlimactic. He had learned so much about his body and how food reacts. He thought he probably could lose weight with the knowledge he had already learned. He couldn't thank the doctors enough. They had changed his life. He and his wife were different people than when they started. Their lives had taken on new meaning. In one sense they owed a part of their lives to these Save Your Life Cholesterol Plan physicians—the longer part they will have to live as a result of the plan

9

How to Lose Excess Weight and Improve Your Image

The time had finally come for the Wilsons to learn some specifics about losing weight on the diet that was already ingrained in their minds. They knew that one out of three adults in this country is obese—a deadly statistic. They also knew the evils of cholesterol; they wouldn't touch an egg if it were thrown at them. They had developed eating habits they never dreamed possible. They were eating complex carbohydrates until it came out their ears. Pasta had become their favorite meal to really fill up on. Snack time had changed drastically. Chocolate was all but eliminated, and cookies a thing of the past. Various kinds of fruit and popcorn were the standard evening snacks.

They no longer kept certain foods around the house; they realized that if food with fat and cholesterol was there, they would eat it. They spent less time thinking about food. They thought a lot less about food and a lot more about being active. Having a steak was a real rarity. They now *saw* the saturated fat in that steak. Baked potatoes without butter were common fare.

They could visualize what happens in the walls of their own arteries whenever the cholesterol intake is elevated. They understood the importance of combating this killer with diet as well as exercise. They appreciated the time spent exercising and all the other pluses achieved with the Save Your Life Cholesterol Plan. They wanted to take what they already knew and apply it to weight control.

Dr. Farris greeted them at his office door.

"I welcome you to your last session of the Save Your Life Cholesterol Plan. I've already heard of your progress to date from the other instructors for the plan. Now I want to give you some ideas about losing the excess weight you are carrying around by applying what you've already learned. My part of the plan is similar to the rest. We'll discuss generalities with a few specifics that must be adhered to in order to make this part of the program successful.

"The overall thesis is what we told you initially: you must utilize more calories than you put into your body. The greater that inverse ratio becomes, the faster you will lose weight. We want you to set a pace that is consistent with your individual life-style. This is not a crash program, but neither is it "a pound a week if you feel like it." We want you to set some goals and persist until you reach them. Each of you will have different diets. One may need to exercise more than the other. One may have to work at not eating more than the other. It is a one-on-one situation. There are no excuses to tell anyone. Either you lose the weight, or you don't. There is no one except yourself to turn to or blame if the weight doesn't come off. The system is tested and proven. So if you accept complete accountability for your success . . . or failure, we will proceed."

"I'm ready." Evelyn took out her notepad once again and prepared to write.

"Let's go with it!" Andy agreed. "I've been ready for this session for a long time. I'm a third of the way to my goal, and you haven't even told us how to lose weight yet."

"Yes, but do you understand why you have already started losing?"

"Sure. It's already been explained that fat contains 9 calories per gram while carbohydrates and proteins contain only 4 per gram. And if I still eat about the same total amount of food but I'm eating carbohydrates and protein, I'm taking in fewer calories on the whole. Plus the exercise program that I've already started.

"Before you move on, I'd like to tell you what has happened to me mentally since I started exercising. Do you mind?" Andy asked.

■ *Diet is the first line of treatment for* <u>*all*</u> *individuals with elevated cholesterol.*

"No, go ahead. I'm glad you're excited."

"One of the doctors said our mental health would improve on this plan. Well, I want to give a testimony to what it has done for me. I found exercise is really an effective means of reducing anxiety and improving self-confidence. My image of myself has improved tremendously; my confidence is so much higher. I really do feel this dieting, and especially the exercising, has a whole lot to do with my overall mental attitude. As I have gotten some of my weight off and started my exercise program, it's so much fun to have all that extra energy.

"One of the reasons I exercise when I come home in the evening is that it restores and rejuvenates me. I have more energy for the evening. I have become good company for my family. I used to be so fatigued when I got home from the office, I flopped down in front of the television with a beer. I just didn't feel like doing anything. I had been nice to everybody all day long, but by evening I didn't feel like being nice to my family. Since I began exercising, something has come alive in me. I have more energy than I ever thought possible. It's a great feeling. Not only am I feeling better, I'm losing some significant weight because of it."

"That's great! You catch on fast. Well, I'm going to tell you how to lose even more weight so you can get down to your goal weight and then rely on your life-style of eating to stay there.

"You will have to learn some calorie counting to do this portion of the plan. We don't require you to carry a book around and add all the calories you eat, but you must have some basic ideas of how many you're eating. We'll set 1000 calories per day for both of you to shoot for. These are relative as you will see. That figure is simply a benchmark for you to keep in mind. I expect men to require several hundred more calories than women, but it will differ tremendously with each individual.

"All I want you to do is become calorie conscious and realize you have to work as hard as you can to lose the weight you have decided to lose. It won't come off easy. It's something you have to work at every minute of the day, every time food enters your mind. You have to go to battle with it until you are conqueror, and your eating habits have turned into a weight loss habit. You will have to dog it to death when you think you are dieting as much as you can and still not losing weight. You have to go back to the simple fact that if you aren't losing weight, evidently you are putting in more than you are making use of.

"The reason we have approached our plan in the order we did is because millions of people have been successful in losing millions of pounds. They have, for the most part, gained it back. Almost anyone can lose weight, but they fail when they begin to put it back on. We have no elite clientele for this plan. We want the average American to understand how to prevent coronary heart disease. You have learned how to keep weight off; now let's learn how to lose it.

"We will discuss weight loss in the extreme, the ultimate

weight loss. It's your choice to what degree you take the program. You may set your pace at three pounds a week, which is a good, steady loss program. Or you may be a little slack and hit one and a half or two pounds a week. It's strictly up to you. I'll tell you how to go all out for it and let you design your own program from there."

Andy interrupted Dr. Farris before he could get started. "One thing I would like to ask about the overall plan. Once I've lost my forty pounds and am at my goal weight, how many calories will I then be able to eat and still hold my weight down?"

"Good question. A lot of my answer depends on how active you stay, how dedicated you are to your exercise program to keep your HDL-C up. So much depends on that. Basically, women average out around 1800 calories a day and men approximately 2300 to maintain the goal weight. But as you can imagine, those numbers are very general. Once you reach your desired weight, I advise you to weigh yourself on the same scales each morning. If for some reason, you have gained a pound, get it off that day. Never let the sun go down on an extra pound. Get it off right now. And the way you do that is to go back to the weight loss part of the plan, which I am about to explain, and stay on it until you are back to your desired weight. Then you can return to your life-style diet maintenance plan.

"It's like keeping a powerful engine finely tuned. You have to keep a close check on it daily and take care of anything that needs correcting that day. There is too great a risk that the pounds can slip up on you. Keep it simple. This is not a controversial program with questionable schemes for losing your weight. It is simply straightforward education by physicians who are summarizing reports from reputable medical journals. The weight maintenance part will be the easiest part of your diet because by that time you will have developed eating habits that will hold you where you are supposed to be. Only when you stray from your habits will you need to make corrections. Understand?"

"Makes sense. Let's go with the weight loss part of the plan. Where do we start?"

"We'll start with the fact that you must cut out everything both you and I consider to be fattening. You don't have to be a dietitian to understand this part of the diet. Decide on these foods immediately and take care of them in your mind right now. Eliminate these foods from your thinking: cookies, all candies, ice cream, cakes, pies, alcohol, potato chips, corn chips, any fried or sweet snack.

"The rule of thumb I stress during the loss part of the diet is simply *no snacks*. That's the rule. If you want to break the rule and eat some fruit or vegetable for a snack, that's up to you. I'm just saying that if you are really serious about meeting your goal in the shortest and safest time period, you will cease to eat snacks. I say shortest and safest period because we don't want you to make this into a crash diet. You need to develop it to suit you. The mind-set should be—no snacks. Make food unimportant in your life for the time being. You will get snacks once you reach the maintenance part of your eating life-style."

"I can handle that." Andy nodded his head in the affirmative. "It's a matter of convincing myself that I will not snack. I can do that. I have that type of persistence."

"Then I suggest you write it down. Write it down on a piece of paper and put it on your mirror or in your pocket or someplace where it will be a constant reminder until you develop the habit of not snacking. There is a certain reinforcement in putting that commitment in writing.

"Next, if you're seriously contemplating going all out in your efforts, go home and throw away all potato chips, Oreo cookies, the little cakes you keep in the cupboard, the bite-sized 150-calorie candy bars you hide in a special place, the M & M's that you save to nibble on just before you go to bed. Put that quart of French vanilla ice cream you just bought into the sink and let it melt. The box of Godiva candy your best friend gave you—you're going to have to let it go, even though you've been eating just one piece at a time. Get rid of all temptations. Do it quickly and all at once. You won't become fainthearted or hypotensive; you will survive. Do it when you first get home. Get them all out of the house—*right now!*"

■ *The goal—PERMANENT CHANGE in eating behavior.*

"We can control the snacks. Now what about our meals?" The commitment was especially difficult for Evelyn because she had such a sweet tooth. No matter how little or how much she ate at a meal, she had always finished with a little something sweet: a few M & M's, a chocolate mint from the restaurant, a bite of cake, or a small candy bar she kept in the refrigerator for special times. But she had convinced herself that it all had to go. She had done the difficult part: the deciding! She decided she wanted to lose weight more than she wanted candy. It was that simple. One or the other—can't have both. She'd weighed it in the balance and made the choice in her mind. She had it licked.

Dr. Farris began. "Breakfast will remain about the same as you've been having. Some type of bran cereal. One difference—use skim milk on your cereal. If you put fruit on it, go sparingly. No toast or jelly, no extras, no frills."

"Just cereal? Nothing else?"

"Two glasses of water will help give you a full feeling and be good for you. I want you to drink six to eight glasses of water a day. Preferably before meals.

"You see, you will use about four ounces of skim milk on your cereal, which gives you around 10 calories per ounce. Add to that 100 to 150 calories for the cereal and you can see that you are under the 200-calorie range and you're off to work with the proper food in your system."

"And lunch?"

"Go back to the basic Save Your Life Cholesterol Plan. The only difference is in amount. The portions must be reduced. Remember to avoid anything fried. Any meat should be broiled and limited to four ounces. Eat baked potato rather than french fries. Salads with little or no dressing. I prefer lemon juice or even a little mustard. Use anything you can come up with other than salad dressing."

Andy had already started adding calories. "How many calories are in the meat and the potato?"

"Figure 50 calories per ounce of lean meat and 100 calories per ounce of fatty meats. So, if you eat four ounces of chicken without the skin and subcutaneous fat attached, you're talking around 200 calories. And that's the type of meat we'll limit you to on this portion of the diet plan."

"Okay, so far I have a 200-calorie breakfast and 200 calories in the meat at lunch." Andy kept adding the calories on his pad.

"Potato, baked—count it at 100 calories," Dr. Farris continued.

"How does that baked potato compare with the same potato as french fries?" Evelyn asked.

"I'm glad for such a practical question. Again a rule of thumb: when you fry a food, multiply by three and you have the supplemented calories. That baked potato cut up and fried would give you about 300 calories. That means for every eight or so fries you eat, you could be eating a whole baked potato."

"It's hard to believe that frying foods can add that many calories."

"Well, look at potato chips. Just eight to ten chips will give you that same 100 calories as your baked potato. The bad part of this story is that we eat french fries and potato chips in addition to our sandwich, so we are just adding 200 calories to what we are eating as the filling portion of the meal. Leave them off and you'll never miss them."

"I've just cut out potato chips and french fries with my lunch . . . in my mind of course." Andy chuckled. "I would have done it long ago if I had known the figures you just gave me. I like baked potatoes for lunch. I used to put gobs of butter or sour cream on them before I started this program. What should I substitute for the condiments?"

"On the weight-loss part of the diet, very little. The less you add, the better. Once you are on maintenance, you can add a little margarine if you have to. Never use butter on potatoes again in your life. Remember butter has the cholesterol; margarine has the same number of calories, but no cholesterol.

"You can add broccoli or mushrooms or some other vegetable to your potato. You will develop a taste for these foods that don't add enough calories even to keep count of. Stir-fry some onions and peppers. You'll find something you like to add. Experiment."

"So we have 200 calories for meat, 100 or so for a baked potato. What about sandwiches, soups, and salads?" Andy was already planning his lunch. If he could figure the calories in what he had just asked about, he could get through 90 percent of any lunch, even the fast-food type he usually eats.

"Okay, let's take those items one at a time. Sandwiches, either the kind you make or the kind you buy. Let's count some baseline calories and get them fixed in your mind. You don't have to know exact numbers, just round figures you can remember. Take a sandwich made with two slices of bread, whole grain if there is a choice, and a piece or two of thin-sliced meat. You can add tomatoes and lettuce for flavor, but you better watch what spread you put on your bread. Keep in mind the 0-15-30 combination when you think of spreads. Mustard has almost no calories, catsup about 15 calories per tablespoon, and mayonnaise 30 calories per teaspoon. Mayonnaise equals butter in my book. We'll give this sandwich a calorie value of 300 to tuck away in your mind.

"Compare that with a fat hamburger with gobs of mayonnaise on it and a slice of cheese. You are easily cutting that in half with your 300-calorie sandwich, and what's the big deal? Which is more important—a little difference in taste satisfaction for ten to fifteen minutes or feeling great and looking better with a healthier, leaner body? Forget the cheese and mayonnaise.

"Next, the salad. You can feel safe with the standard garden salad of lettuce, tomatoes, cucumbers, celery, cauliflower, broccoli, mushrooms, and the like with a calorie count in the 50 to 100 range. The problem is all the extras at salad bars these days. You can pile on items that really add up the calories without your realizing what you're doing. Most of these extras do not add cholesterol, but they do add calories. As long as you are on the weight-loss portion of your diet, you have to be cognizant of what adds calories. A bean and vegetable salad raises the calories to the 300 range. A serving of chicken salad will hit 200, while potato salad with hardcooked eggs and mayonnaise dressing exceeds 350 calories per serving. You've already heard that if you use the Thousand Island dressing that comes with a McDonald's salad, the dressing will make the salad end up with more calories than a Big Mac.

"What ruins the garden salad as a basic diet meal for most people is the indiscriminate use of dressing on the salad. Using two tablespoons as the average amount, we see that blue cheese and Roquefort cheese dressings add 150 calories, while the national dressings of French, Italian, and Russian are right behind at 135 to 145. Thousand Island isn't much better at 120 calories.

"The low-calorie dressings are an improvement. Blue cheese drops to the 20-calorie range, and French, Italian, Russian, and Thousand Island hit the 40-calorie range, and some dressings are in the 6- to 8-calorie range. Wishbone is making light dressings in this very low category.

"Even better yet is simply to use lemon juice or cut down your low-calorie dressing to only one tablespoon. The important factor to remember is that you can multiply the calories you are eating sixfold by adding salad dressing. In general, think of even low-calorie dressing as adding significant calories to what you are taking in."

"Blue cheese is my favorite dressing." Andy's slight frown changed to a smile. "I first thought I would have to give it up until you mentioned those low-calorie dressings. Blue cheese hit the bottom mark with 20. I can live with that any day."

■ *Establishing a desirable body weight may completely correct an elevated cholesterol. Commit to diet.*

"I'll tell you what I've just realized about the salads I've been eating," Evelyn added. "When I go through a salad bar, I usually add the beans and potato salad on the side of my plate. I'll simply cut those out until I reach my goal weight since they add so much to my calorie count."

"Great. You both have caught on quickly. That leaves only soups on the list before we discuss your evening meal.

"We will go over some specific soups in a minute, but let's lump them together at 100 calories per cup. There's a wide variation, but for general use, learn that base number. Add about 75 calories to that number if you use milk rather than water in the soup.

"You will also need to remember that we're talking cups rather than bowls. On the weight-loss part of your program, limit soup to a cup rather than a bowl. Avoid the milk-based soups if you have a choice; milk base almost doubles the calories.

"Now for some specifics, we'll look at the more common soups. You can add your favorites to the base list as we go along. Using water as a base, the 100-calorie soups include cream of celery, cream of mushroom, New England clam chowder, chicken noodle, tomato, and vegetable beef. The broths drop down to the 25-calorie range. The higher calorie soups include any of the above if milk is used as a base. In the 150-calorie range we find chili beef made with water, green pea soup made with water, and cream of potato made with milk."

Andy began to add up calories for a lunch that included soup. "So far, on the weight-loss part of the plan when I am really hitting my all-time low in calories I can afford to eat, I have my basic cereal breakfast at 200 calories. Then I move on to lunch where I can choose from a sandwich at 300 calories, four ounces of skinless chicken at 200 calories, a baked potato at 100 calories, a garden salad rounded off at 100 calories, or soup at 100 calories.

"All I have to remember for lunch is 100, 200, or 300. I'm already learning to think like you doctors—keep it simple. The 100-calorie list includes soup, salad, or potato. The 200-calorie group includes the lean meats of chicken or fish, and the 300-calorie group has sandwiches of the leanest, thinnest kind. Today I think I would rather have a baked potato and small salad and save a few extra calories for dinner."

"Excellent. I like the way you think."

Evelyn wanted to know what to do about the drinks with lunch.

"Water is always your basic drink with every meal. Some people prefer unsweetened iced tea, some even a diet cola. leave that up to you as long as you don't add significant calories to your meal; but think water and drink plenty of it. You'l feel full, and it has zero calories."

"What if you eat your main meal in the middle of the da and your light meal in the evening?" Evelyn asked.

"Just reverse your guidelines for lunch with those for dinner. Simple as that. But let me give you a bit of advice about eating your large meal in the middle of the day. I strongly advise against it for the simple reason of the evening hours ahead. If you eat your greatest amount at noontime and a light evening meal, you are going to get hungry, very hungry before bedtime. You'll have a battle on your hands every night to keep from giving in and eating before going to bed. For that reason, I suggest you eat lightly at noon and have your full meal in the evenings. But if you go out for lunch and eat a full meal, then, right then, decide to eat a light supper that evening. Never eat two large meals the same day.

"Now, let's go on to those dinner guidelines and see how you can control your daily eating habits to hit the 1000-calorie mark." Dr. Farris pulled out another sheet of instructions from his top desk drawer. He felt very good about how responsive his two patients had been so far. He was about ready to turn them loose to become different people.

"Implementing this last phase of the daily program can be expedited by reviewing your exercise instructions. Exercise seems to diminish appetite in many people. We think it's related to the fact that when you exercise, you release epinephrine into your system, which in turn promotes gluconeogenesis—the breakdown of stored glycogen into glucose. When the level of glucose in your blood is low, you become hungry; and vice versa, when the level is high, your hunger is diminished. If your schedule permits, do your exercising prior to eating your evening meal. Your hunger will not be as great, and you will tend to eat less. This can give you a little extra edge, especially for the weight-reduction portion of your program.

"I want to give you one other bit of advice. Don't skip any meals thinking you are cutting out a portion of your daily intake. If you cut out breakfast and make it on a fairly slim lunch, by dinnertime you are famished and become much less able to control what you eat at that time. It has been shown that people who diet by skipping meals end up not losing weight and many times they actually gain."

Dr. Farris continued giving advice, sharing all the secrets he knew to help the couple in the weight-loss part of the diet. He knew the Save Your Life Cholesterol Plan is unprecedented in its comprehensive presentation of our number one health problem.

"The major aspect of the weight-loss part of the plan is cutting down on fat and meat and increasing the complex carbohydrates. You must replace your meats and fats with potatoes, beans, vegetables, and fruits. During this weight-loss phase, you must go all out to remain aware of everything you eat. You must realize how many extra calories and how much saturated fat you are eating at dinnertime when you order that steak and salad with blue cheese dressing and that baked potato drowning in butter.

"Eat meat only as a condiment, just to flavor your food. For two to three days a week leave meat out entirely. When you do eat meat, choose poultry with the skin removed or fish. Vegetables are more important during this phase; eat them at both dinner and lunch. Fresh fruit will become commonplace on the dinner table. You will have no desserts during this time except for the fruit. This will help you form the habit of eating fruit rather than pies and cakes later in the program.

"During this phase, you need to avoid fried foods like the plague. You can charcoal your chicken and bake your fish. Your main dinner course will center on vegetables, beans, and grains. You will be eating more pasta, rice, cereals, breads and potatoes, peas and beans."

Andy looked up from his writing long enough to ask for some details. "I've been counting calories ever since I came in here. How about giving me some numbers I can remember for all these dinner foods you're throwing at us."

"Okay, I'll give you some numbers to go by. These calorie totals are measured per cup of vegetable, but remember that many times, the average portion of one vegetable may be only one-half or three-fourths a cup. The calories per cup standard gives you a better means of comparing one vegetable with another. I'll stick to the more common vegetables most people eat. If you want to know exact calories for almost any food or combination of foods, buy Bowes and Church's *Food Values of Portions Commonly Used*. It gives very complete data on the nutrient values of almost any food you can think of.

"Let's start with a serving of white corn at 175 calories per cup or a four-inch ear of corn on the cob at 100.

■ *Saturated fats raise the total blood cholesterol.*

"For beans, you can have green beans at a low of 30, kidney beans at a high of 300, or white beans at 250. Lima beans are 175. Black-eyed peas are a close first cousin at 150 calories per cup, and even lower are green peas at 100, but who can eat a cup of green peas?

"We've already talked about the excellent baked potato at 100 calories, although a cup of creamed potatoes hits the 150 range; and frying the potato brings it on up to 250. Scalloped potatoes are also 250 calories per cup. The highest total for potatoes is in potato salad with mayonnaise at 350 calories a cup. That gives you a guideline for your potatoes.

"White rice is a good alternative at 200. Fried rice moves up to the 300-calorie range."

"So," Andy interrupted, "the next time I'm at a restaurant and the waitress asks if I want rice pilaf or baked potato, I'll take the 100-calorie potato rather than the 200-calorie cup of rice."

"Yes, especially on this weight-loss part of your diet. Let's continue with our list.

"A baked sweet potato is around 200 calories, while a cup of candied yams at near 400 almost doubles the total."

"Baked potato, 100; sweet potato doubles to 200; candied yams doubles to 400," Evelyn verbalized her notes. "I know potatoes now.

"I've heard about some vegetables with very low calorie counts. What are some of those?" She wanted to know which vegetables she could fill up on without adding calories.

"Yes, there are quite a few of those. When adding up calories, you can almost ignore most of these. Remember, I'm giving you calories per cup and you use many of these vegetables only as condiments so you can eat a lot without adding many calories. Vegetables that fall in the 50-calorie range include broccoli, carrots, onions, mushrooms, beets, and radishes. If we drop to the 25-calorie-per-cup group, we find cauliflower, lettuce, bell pepper, celery, and cabbage."

"That's about enough for me." Andy was tired of writing numbers on his tablet. If he could just learn the calories he had written down, he would have a good base to go by. For any other foods he wants to know about, he can go to the library and look them up or order the book Dr. Farris had mentioned. "I think I can intelligently aim for the 1000-calorie mark each day with what you have given us. I can keep breakfast at 200 calories with cereal and skim milk. I can hold lunch at the 200 to 300 range with soups, salads, baked potatoes, or half-sandwiches. That will leave me close to 500 for dinner when I'll eat some chicken or fish occasionally, lots of vegetables, and the complex carbohydrates like pasta, potatoes, cereals, bread, beans, and rice."

"Good! You're on the right track. Remember, this program is aimed not at restricting calories per se, but at eating foods that are lower in fat content and don't have such a high calorie count per bite. As you recall, there are 9 calories in each gram of fat and only 4 in carbohydrates and protein. I like to think of it as more than twice the number of calories per bite of fatty

foods as compared to a bite of complex carbohydrates or vegetables. We want to develop a life-style habit of eating fewer
foods that contain fats and more foods that consist of fiber and
complex carbohydrates. The only time you will have to really
keep up with the number of calories you are eating is during
this weight-loss part of the Save Your Life Cholesterol Plan. By
the time you reach your goal weight, you won't have to count
calories in everything you eat. You will have the habit of not
eating foods with cholesterol and saturated fats and of rou-
tinely eating the proper foods for good health and a trim body.

"Now, as I finish up on the last segment of the weight-loss
portion of the program, I want your undivided attention. This
part is imperative. If you are serious about losing weight, you
must commit to what I am about to stress with you. During the
weight-loss part of your Save Your Life Cholesterol Plan, you
must exercise. Exercise is the single most important factor in
losing weight. It is essential in balancing your muscle mass
with the rest of your body to give you the best-looking body
you can develop.

"If you are not going to commit to a daily exercise program
with a minimum of five days a week, you will be fighting an
uphill battle from the beginning. You will lose some weight,
but you will not reach your full potential in the weight-loss
part of the program. I ask you to make that commitment and to
start on it today."

"What kind of exercise are you talking about?" Evelyn was
taken aback by the emphasis Dr. Farris was giving to exercise.

"The kind of exercise I'm talking about will be different for
you and your husband, but it will have the same goal. I'm talking about regular activity thirty minutes a day, to the point that
your heart rate is elevated to 70 to 80 percent maximum. This
is best done by using your large muscle mass, actually moving
your entire body. The most effective such exercises include
walking, jogging, bicycle riding, rowing, swimming, jumping
rope, and similar total body exercises.

"I want you to commit today, right now, to an exercise program. Remember, I'm not Dr. Lamm. I'm not the exercise doctor, but I feel just as strongly about this point."

He looked at Evelyn. "You may want to start with walking. You may start out at a slow pace, but stretch your leg muscles for four or five minutes before you start and after you finish. The stretching time does not count in your thirty minutes of exercise. Dr. Lamm described your stretching routine; I'll reiterate how important I think it is. Review what he taught you about stretching and adhere to it."

Dr. Farris looked toward Andy next. "You look like you could begin with jogging. You may have to work up to it but at least commit to doing it. The before and after stretching will be even more important for you. You may start at a slow pace and up the intensity as time goes by. You may end up walking for the last portion of your time, but you will need to decrease the walking segment until you are really exerting yourself fully. Some days, you may elect to play tennis or racquetball, but you should work at it as an exercise rather than a sport during this part of the diet program. By that I mean you need to play continuously without the usual rest periods. Find someone who is also willing to play the sport primarily for exercise. The game will have to move, move, move. You can also hit the swimming pool occasionally. Just remember, your exercise needs to be continuous rather than start and stop.

"I am going to turn you both loose and let you begin becoming the individuals you have kept hidden inside for so many years. The Save Your Life Cholesterol Plan is made for individuals who have shown dissatisfaction with the way they look, with what they weigh, and with how they take care of their bodies. You both exemplify such individuals. I can assure you success because I know your commitment. I can assure you a change in your overall outlook on yourself. You will feel a sense of control of your life, a new feeling of satisfaction.

"And best of all, you will develop a life-style of eating that will not only help prevent the number one killer disease in America, but the years you do live will be healthy ones that you can enjoy as you utilize to its fullest potential the body that God has given you.

"I wish you wellness and the greatest possible life you can live. As motivational teacher and author Zig Ziglar says, 'I'll see you at the top.'"

APPENDIX A

SAVE YOUR LIFE TEST

(Answers immediately follow the test.)

1. What one disease kills more Americans than any other disease, including all forms of cancer put together?

   _____

2. What are the three main causes of coronary heart disease (heart attacks)?

   (1) _____

   (2) _____

   (3) _____

3. Is it a proven fact that high levels of cholesterol in the blood increase your risk for a heart attack?

   ☐ yes   ☐ no

4. Can you decrease your chances of having a heart attack by eating less cholesterol and saturated fat?

   ☐ yes   ☐ no

5. What percentage of Americans have cholesterol levels that put them at an increased risk of coronary heart disease?

   ☐ 10 percent
   ☐ 20 percent
   ☐ greater than 50 percent

189

6. What three foods make up 90 percent of the cholesterol you eat?

   (1) _____ _____ percent

   (2) _____ _____ percent

   (3) _____ _____ percent

7. Why is high blood-cholesterol known as "the silent killer"?

_____

8. What are the five most commonly eaten "killer foods"?

   (1) _____

   (2) _____

   (3) _____

   (4) _____

   (5) _____

9. Which cholesterol is considered "bad"?

_____

   Which cholesterol is considered "good"?

_____

10. If a male of normal weight exercises regularly and has a total cholesterol level of 200, does that mean he is risk-free of developing coronary heart disease?

   ☐ yes   ☐ no

11. Is too little HDL-cholesterol as dangerous as too much LDL-cholesterol?

   ☐ yes   ☐ no

12. What are the eight risk factors, other than an elevated level of LDL-cholesterol, of which any two will place you in a high-risk status for having coronary heart disease?

   (1) _____

   (2) _____

   (3) _____

   (4) _____

   (5) _____

(6) _____

(7) _____

(8) _____

13. What is the safe range of total cholesterol if you have no additional risk factors for coronary heart disease?

_____

14. What is the lower limit for "good" HDL-cholesterol, below which is considered a definite risk factor for developing coronary heart disease?

_____

15. What are the three main dietary habits that contribute most to elevating your cholesterol?

(1) _____

(2) _____

(3) _____

16. If a sixty-five-year-old has already had a heart attack, will lowering his/her cholesterol now help prevent a second heart attack later?

☐ yes   ☐ no

17. What is the cornerstone of treatment for controlling your cholesterol?

_____

18. What is the best nonmedicated means of raising your HDL-cholesterol?

_____

19. What should you do to ensure your best chances for controlling cholesterol and avoiding a heart attack?

(1) _____

(2) _____

(3) _____

(4) _____

(5) _____

20. In general, which foods should you eat to lower your cholesterol?

    _____

    In general, which foods should you avoid to lower your cholesterol?

    _____

21. Chicken and beef have similar amounts of cholesterol. So far as coronary heart disease is concerned, why is chicken better for you to eat than beef?

    _____

    _____

    _____

    _____

22. At what age does cholesterol begin to be laid down in the walls of the arteries of your heart?

    _____

    _____

23. Some people have cholesterol problems because of their genetic makeup—and there is nothing they can do about it.
    ☐ yes   ☐ no

24. Individuals who exercise regularly are protected from cholesterol problems and coronary heart disease.
    ☐ yes   ☐ no

25. How important is oat bran in preventing coronary heart disease?

    _____

    _____

26. Does a high fiber diet have any direct affect on your cholesterol?

    _____

    _____

27. Are there any foods that contain "good" HDL-cholesterol?
    ☐ yes   ☐ no

28. Most of the cholesterol found in your blood consists of the "bad" LDL-cholesterol.

☐ yes   ☐ no

29. What is the correlation between LDL-cholesterol and HDL-cholesterol in coronary heart disease?

_____

_____

30. Saturated fat and cholesterol in the diet both affect blood-cholesterol levels. Which of the two has greater influence?

_____

_____

_____

31. Is obesity related to having high blood-cholesterol?

_____

_____

Answers

1. Coronary heart disease kills more Americans than any other disease, including all forms of cancer put together. In coronary heart disease, the arteries to the heart are blocked, which leads to a heart attack.

2. (1) Elevated blood-cholesterol
   (2) Smoking
   (3) High blood pressure

3. Yes. The National Cholesterol Education Program states that the risk of having a heart attack rises progressively with cholesterol level, particularly when cholesterol levels rise above 200 mg/dl.

4. Yes. Studies have shown that for individuals with cholesterol levels initially above 250, each 1 percent reduction in their cholesterol resulted in approximately 2 percent reduction in coronary heart disease rates. This means if you have a cholesterol

level of 250 and drop it to 200, you would reduce your chance of coronary heart disease by approximately 40 percent.

5. Greater than 50 percent.

6. (1) Eggs   40 percent
       (approximately half hidden in cooked foods)
   (2) Red meat   30 percent
   (3) Dairy products   20 percent
       (approximately half is from whole milk)

7. High blood-cholesterol is known as "the silent killer" because you may have absolutely no symptoms prior to a fatal heart attack. The first symptom of 18 percent of Americans who have heart attacks is death. Cholesterol can kill without warning. It can definitely be a silent killer with no warning at all. You can be a marathon runner in great shape yet have an elevated cholesterol count and suddenly die from coronary heart disease. You should know your cholesterol level.

8. In order of consumption:
   (1) Egg yolk
   (2) Red meat
   (3) Whole milk
   (4) Cheese
   (5) Butter

9. LDL-cholesterol (low-density lipoprotein-cholesterol) is considered "bad."
   HDL-cholesterol (high-density lipoprotein-cholesterol) is considered "good."

10. No. His "good" high-density lipoprotein-cholesterol (HDL-cholesterol) may be abnormally low, or he may have another associated risk factor related to coronary heart disease. Being a male is one additional risk factor in itself.

11. Yes. Studies are now stressing the dangerous significance of a low HDL-cholesterol. In one thousand patients hospitalized for chest pain, one-third were found to have normal total cholesterol levels. Of these patients, two-thirds of the men had low HDL-cholesterol, and four-fifths of the women. HDL-cholesterol

levels do not show up on screening tests of total cholesterol alone.

12. (1) Being male
    (2) Having low HDL-cholesterol
    (3) Smoking cigarettes
    (4) Having hypertension
    (5) Being obese
    (6) Having a family history of heart attack before age fifty-five
    (7) Having diabetes
    (8) Having a history of blockage of the arteries to the brain or legs

13. Below 200 is desirable blood-cholesterol. Having a cholesterol level of 240 mg/dl almost doubles your coronary heart disease risk as compared to a level of 200 mg/dl.

14. Anything below 35 is considered a coronary heart disease risk factor. Normal HDL-cholesterol level for men is 40 to 50; normal HDL-cholesterol level for women is 50 to 60.

15. (1) High intake of foods containing cholesterol
    (2) High intake of foods containing saturated fatty acids
    (3) A generalized high caloric intake which commonly leads to obesity

16. Yes. Findings in the medical literature strongly suggest that lowering your LDL-cholesterol will be as effective in preventing a second heart attack and/or death as it would be in preventing a first occurrence. That is the reason it is so important for everyone who has ever had coronary heart disease to understand how to beat the cholesterol problem and reduce the chance of having subsequent heart attacks.

17. Diet modification is the primary approach that should lead to a permanent change in eating habits. Even if you are placed on cholesterol-lowering medication, diet remains the primary cholesterol-control program.

18. Vigorous exercise has been shown to increase HDL-cholesterol. The best studies advise thirty minutes of continuous exercise, five days a week, in which your heart rate is elevated to the 75

percent increase range of your maximum heart rate. Avoidance of both smoking and obesity also affects your HDL-cholesterol favorably. Exercise will lower triglycerides, will raise HDL-cholesterol, and may lower the LDL-cholesterol.

19. (1) Have your cholesterol checked and discuss the results with your physician.
    (2) Set goals in your mind to develop your body into physiological excellence.
    (3) Develop a thorough understanding of the response of your body to cholesterol and saturated fats.
    (4) Develop your own permanent personal life-style of eating that consists of a diet low in cholesterol and saturated fats and high in complex carbohydrates and fiber.
    (5) Devise a personal exercise program designed for your life-style.

20. You should eat foods high in carbohydrates and fiber and decrease foods high in cholesterol, fats (especially saturated fats), and total calories.

	CHOOSE	DECREASE
Fish, chicken, turkey, and lean meats	Fish, poultry without skin, lean cuts of beef, lamb, pork or veal, shellfish	Fatty cuts of beef, lamb, pork, spare ribs, organ meats, regular cold cuts, sausage, hot dogs, bacon, sardines, roe
Skim and low-fat milk, cheese, yogurt, and dairy substitutes	Skim or 1% fat milk (liquid, powdered, evaporated), buttermilk	Whole milk (4% fat); regular, evaporated, condensed; cream, half and half, 2% milk, imitation milk products, most nondairy creamers, whipped toppings
	Nonfat (0% fat) or low-fat yogurt	Whole-milk yogurt
	Low-fat cottage cheese (1% or 2% fat)	Whole-milk cottage cheese (4% fat)

	Low-fat cheeses, farmer or pot cheeses (all of these should be labeled no more than 2–6 g fat/ounce)	All natural cheeses (e.g., blue, roquefort, camembert, cheddar, swiss)
		Low-fat or "light" cream cheese, low-fat or "light" sour cream
	Sherbet, sorbet	Ice cream
Eggs	Egg whites (2 whites = 1 whole egg in recipes), cholesterol-free egg substitutes	Egg yolks
Fruits and vegetables	Fresh, frozen, canned, or dried fruits and vegetables	Vegetables prepared in butter, cream, or other sauces
Breads and cereals	Homemade baked goods using unsaturated oils sparingly, angel food cake, low-fat crackers, low-fat cookies	Commercial baked goods; pies, cakes, doughnuts, croissants, pastries, muffins, biscuits, high-fat crackers, high-fat cookies
	Rice, pasta	Egg noodles
	Whole-grain breads and cereals (oatmeal, whole wheat, rye, bran, multigrain, etc.)	Breads in which eggs are a major ingredient
Fats and oils	Baking cocoa	Chocolate
	Unsaturated vegetable oils; corn, olive, rapeseed (canola oil), safflower, sesame, soybean, sunflower	Butter, coconut oil, palm oil, palm kernel oil, lard, bacon fat
	Margarine or shortening made from one of the unsaturated oils listed above	
	Diet margarine	

Mayonnaise, salad dressings made with unsaturated oils listed above	Dressings made with egg yolk
Low-fat dressings	
Seeds and nuts	Coconut

SOURCE: The U.S. Department of Health and Human Services National Cholesterol Education Program.

21. Two main factors affect the level of cholesterol in your bloodstream: the amount of cholesterol in your diet and the amount of saturated fat. Saturated fat has a direct effect on your cholesterol level and causes it to become elevated. Saturated fats need to be viewed on equal basis as cholesterol. One ounce of beef has 27 milligrams of cholesterol; one ounce of chicken has 26. However, when comparing the saturated fat content of the two, we find up to 4.8 grams of saturated fat in beef but only 0.5 grams in the chicken. Beef can have three to nine times the saturated fat as chicken. Think of saturated fat as being cholesterol's first cousin.

22. A revealing article, "Coronary Artery Disease in Combat Casualties in Vietnam," in the *Journal of the American Medical Association* reported on 105 American soldiers killed in action. Their mean age was 22.1 years. Forty-five percent of the soldiers examined had some degree of atherosclerosis (blockage) in one or more of their coronary arteries. Even more alarming was the fact that 25 percent of them had involvement of at least two of the three main arteries of the heart. At a recent medical meeting, Dr. Robert Jones, a cardiac surgeon at Duke Medical School, stated that the process of atherosclerosis begins in our teenage years. Some reports in the medical literature place it even earlier. Proper eating habits in relation to cholesterol and saturated fats should be taught to our young people prior to the age of 22.1 years.

23. No. Our genetic makeup does play a role in how our bodies handle cholesterol, but that is no reason to become complacent with our cholesterol levels. Of individuals who have genetic traits that cause them to have elevated cholesterol, less than 10

percent will need medication for treating the disorder. Numerous studies indicate that sensible eating and exercise remain the chief strongholds in controlling cholesterol. This is true even if medication is required.

24. No. An article in the *New England Journal of Medicine* reviewed 47 studies concerning physical activity and coronary heart disease. Sixty-eight percent of these studies showed a statistically significant inverse association between physical activity and coronary heart disease. The more exercise, the less coronary heart disease seen. Exercise alone does not eliminate the risk of coronary heart disease, however. Cholesterol, smoking, and high blood pressure remain the leading causes of heart attacks and these three factors have to be taken into account. It is possible to exercise daily and yet have an elevated cholesterol count that results in a heart attack.

25. According to a study in the *American Journal of Cardiology*, documented cases around the world suggest that eating a significant amount of oat bran, oatmeal, or beans could help to protect against coronary heart disease. Some reports show as high as 20 to 25 percent decrease in total cholesterol. It is important to realize that oat bran is not a panacea but is only one piece of a complex puzzle relating to the control of cholesterol.

26. There are two basic types of fiber: one is water soluble and the other water insoluble. Water-soluble fiber affects your cholesterol favorably. The two main ones are oat bran and beans. Water-insoluble fiber gives bulk and plays a significant role in decreasing the chances of developing colon cancer, diverticulosis, diverticulitis, and other related colon diseases, but it doesn't have a significant effect on cholesterol. The most common form of water-insoluble fiber is found in wheat.

27. No. HDL-cholesterol is a combination of cholesterol and protein. It is probably produced in the liver. HDL-cholesterol is looked upon as protective against heart attacks. HDL-C below 35 mg/dl is considered a significant risk factor for developing coronary heart disease. Exercise, cessation of smoking, and correction of obesity will help in increasing your HDL-C.

28. Yes. Approximately 50 to 70 percent of the circulating cholesterol in the blood is in the LDL-cholesterol faction. In contrast, only about 25 percent of the total cholesterol found is "good" HDL-cholesterol.

29. The higher the levels of LDL-cholesterol, the greater the risk of developing coronary heart disease. In contrast, the higher the level of HDL-cholesterol, the lesser the risk of coronary heart disease.

30. Excess cholesterol in the diet appears to raise LDL-cholesterol levels in the blood. However, the effect of cholesterol is not as predictable as that of saturated fats. Saturated fats raise total blood cholesterol levels and, especially, LDL-cholesterol. Saturated fatty acids have the greatest influence on blood cholesterol than any other foods in the diet. It is important to know which foods contain the greatest amounts of saturated fats as well as the greatest amounts of cholesterol. The most common foods containing saturated fats are red meats and the dairy products: whole milk, cream, ice cream, butter, and cheese. Coconut oil and palm oil are also high in saturated fat as well as many bakery products, snack foods, and convenience foods.

31. Obesity is associated with an elevated LDL-cholesterol. Reducing your weight may lower your LDL-cholesterol as well as reducing your triglycerides and raising your HDL-cholesterol. Exercise is an important aid in weight reduction. Regular exercise will burn up calories and decrease your appetite as well as raising HDL-cholesterol and lowering triglycerides. In some people, reduction to a normal body weight will completely correct their elevated LDL-cholesterol. Weight reduction to a normal range should be an integral part of cholesterol control.

APPENDIX B

SAVE YOUR LIFE FACTS

WHY IS CHOLESTEROL BAD?

Almost 5.5 million Americans have symptoms of coronary heart disease, of which 1.5 million result in heart attacks, with one-third of those ending in death. More Americans die from coronary heart disease than all forms of cancer combined. Approximately 50 percent of Americans die from some form of cardiovascular disease.

Coronary Heart Disease: Number One Killer in America

Many millions more of us have plugged arteries of our hearts but remain undiagnosed because this disease many times progresses silently, with no warning signs prior to a heart attack.

Even more alarming are reports that up to 75 percent of males and 60 percent of females may have cholesterol higher than desired levels. Your best defense against this dreaded disease process is prevention.

The Causes of Heart Attacks

The three main causative factors of coronary heart disease are (1) elevated blood-cholesterol, (2) smoking, and (3) hypertension. All three are controllable. Hypertension can be controlled pharmacologically, smoking can be avoided, and 90 percent of Americans can reduce their cholesterol to acceptable levels through diet and exercise without dependence on prescription drugs. An elevated level of cholesterol in the blood is a proven major cause of coronary heart disease.

Cholesterol is essential in making cell membranes in our bodies and in producing hormones; it is a precursor of bile acids that are produced in the liver and secreted into the intestines to aid in digestion. Approximately 60 to 80 percent of our cholesterol is manufactured in the body, with the remainder coming from our diet. If more is taken in by means of our food than the liver can control, then high blood-cholesterol results. Diet is the controllable factor in determining the cholesterol level.

HOW CHOLESTEROL AFFECTS YOUR HEART

It has been medically established that increased blood levels of "bad" cholesterol, LDL-cholesterol, result in an increased risk of coronary heart disease. This risk of a heart attack increases as the cholesterol level rises, especially when the total cholesterol level rises above 200 mg/dl.

Cholesterol and the Rest of the World

Much evidence reveals that populations throughout the world who have elevated total cholesterol levels also have a higher number of heart attacks than populations with low cholesterol. If individuals who have low total cholesterols migrate to a country that has higher cholesterols in its population—and they acquire the eating habits of their new country—their cholesterol levels and coronary heart disease rates will progress toward those of their new country.

The medical literature accepts the cause-and-effect relationship that elevated blood-cholesterol increases the risk of having a heart attack. The higher the cholesterol level, the greater the risk.

Lowering Cholesterol Lowers Risk of Heart Attacks

More important, medical trials have shown this risk can be lowered by lowering one's LDL-cholesterol. A most significant study on individuals whose cholesterol levels were between 250 and 300 mg/dl showed that for each 1 percent reduction in serum-cholesterol level, there was approximately a 2 percent reduction in coronary heart disease.

We must accept these important medical findings and develop personal eating habits and exercise programs to help prevent this disease process from becoming the cause of our demise.

WHAT YOUR TOTAL CHOLESTEROL COUNT REALLY MEANS

It is recommended that all persons over age 20 have cholesterol levels checked as part of routine medical examinations. A thorough knowledge of the breakdown of your total cholesterol count is imperative in understanding and controlling your cholesterol.

Most screening tests provide only the *total cholesterol*. The National Cholesterol Education Program, which is coordinated by the National Heart, Lung, and Blood Institute, the U.S. Dept. of Health and Human Services, the Public Health Services, and the National Institutes of Health, has devised three risk categories based on the total cholesterol level:

1. Those whose total cholesterol is less than 200 mg/dl are deemed to have "desirable blood-cholesterol."
2. Total cholesterol of 200 to 239 mg/dl indicates "borderline high blood-cholesterol."
3. Total cholesterol over 240 mg/dl means individuals have "high blood-cholesterol."

This approach to screening, however, does not provide any information concerning the specific amounts of "good" cholesterol (HDL-cholesterol) or "bad" cholesterol (LDL-cholesterol).

The National Cholesterol Education Program recommends that persons in all categories be given dietary education designed to lower cholesterol. It recommends blood tests that break down the total cholesterol into its subcomponents of the "bad" LDL-cholesterol and the "good" HDL-cholesterol if the total cholesterol is in the "high blood-cholesterol" category of greater than 240 mg/dl.

The program also recommends this breakdown of total cholesterol for an individual in the "borderline high blood-cholesterol" category who has known coronary heart disease or any two of the following risk factors:

1. Being male
2. Having a family history of definite heart attack or sudden death before age 55
3. Smoking cigarettes
4. Having high blood pressure
5. Having low HDL-cholesterol (below 35 mg/dl)
6. Having diabetes
7. Having a history of definite disease of the arteries to the brain or legs
8. Being obese—more than 30 percent overweight

To understand cholesterol well enough to develop proper eating habits, you need to look at the breakdown of your total cholesterol. This reading can be envisioned by the following modified formula:

$$\text{Total cholesterol} = (\text{LDL-cholesterol}) + (\text{HDL-cholesterol}) + (\text{triglycerides}/5)$$

You want to lower your "bad" LDL-cholesterol and raise your "good" HDL-cholesterol.

The National Cholesterol Education Program further classifies cholesterol levels based on the "bad" LDL-cholesterol:

1. LDL-cholesterol of less than 130 indicates "desirable LDL-cholesterol."
2. LDL-cholesterol of 130 to 159 points to "borderline high-risk LDL-cholesterol."

3. LDL-cholesterol of more than 160 means "high-risk LDL-cholesterol."

THE EFFECTS OF "BAD" LDL-CHOLESTEROL AND "GOOD" HDL-CHOLESTEROL ON YOUR HEART

When you think of foods containing cholesterol, consider saturated fat as cholesterol's twin because an increase in saturated fat consumption results in an increased cholesterol level in the blood. After cholesterol is ingested and enters the bloodstream, it is enveloped by protein and is transported through the blood in this protein-cholesterol combination. In understanding the physiology of cholesterol, you must comprehend the two major protein-cholesterol combinations.

The "bad" cholesterol is the low-density lipoprotein-cholesterol combination. The "good" cholesterol is the high-density lipoprotein-cholesterol combination. These two types of cholesterol are termed LDL-cholesterol and HDL-cholesterol respectively. The "bad" LDL-cholesterol actually enters the walls of your arteries, leading to blockage of blood flow. The "good" HDL-cholesterol somehow acts as a scavenger, being responsible for the removal of "bad" LDL-cholesterol and transportation of it to the liver for disposal.

There is no food that actually contains HDL-cholesterol. It is not something you can eat that raises your HDL-cholesterol, but a physiological process in your body causes an increase in your "good" HDL-cholesterol.

HOW TO REDUCE YOUR CHOLESTEROL

Diet is the cornerstone for controlling your cholesterol. The goal is to maintain good nutrition while reversing the trend of eating excess cholesterol and saturated fat. Remember that the body can make both saturated fatty acids and cholesterol in abundance. Neither is essential in one's diet; the real need is to reduce the intake of both these food sources.

Follow the Recommended Diet

The recommended diet of the National Cholesterol Education Program is initially to decrease the amount of total fat to less than 30 percent of your total calories, with saturated fatty acids being less than 10 percent of your total calories in your diet. The remainder of your diet would consist of 50 to 60 percent of your calories as carbohydrates, 10 to 20 percent as protein, and cholesterol limited to less than 300 mg/day.

Change Your Eating Habits

This recommended diet can be nutritionally adequate, but many times it is difficult to know all the percentages of the specific foods you eat each day. It is important to realize that you cannot think of your goal as some sort of temporary diet. You must think of it as a permanent change in your eating habits. You must develop a habit of eating less saturated fats and cholesterol. You need to learn which foods contain these substances and avoid them. At the same time, learn to substitute complex carbohydrates, fruit, and fiber.

Develop a Practical Diet

Practically speaking, you should avoid or completely eliminate certain foods. There has to be a permanent change in the typical diet of the average American. Some practical changes you can make are based on the elimination of foods high in cholesterol, saturated fats, and total fats.

FOODS TO ELIMINATE AND SUBSTITUTE

Commonly eaten foods high in cholesterol and saturated fats include the following:

1. Eggs
2. Red meat
3. Whole milk
4. Cheese
5. Butter

Memorize this list of foods and make substitutions in your diet. This is a practical first step in permanently changing your eating habits.

1. *Eggs*. Completely eliminate eating known eggs. There will be eggs used in cooking that you will not know about. Substitute two egg whites for one whole egg in cooking.

Substitution food. Bran cereal for breakfast, with fruit and 1 percent or skim milk.

2. *Red meat*. Make a concerted effort to avoid red meat. Avoid ordering or cooking steaks, veal, or pork. Do not let hamburgers be your standard fast-food order.

Substitution foods. Chicken, turkey, and fish are the most common substitutions. Most of the fat in chicken occurs just under and attached to the skin.

3. *Whole milk*. Simply quit drinking whole milk, which is approximately 4 percent fat. Eliminate ice cream from your eating habits.

Substitution foods. Buy skim milk or 1 percent milk for use at home. What you have at home will become a standard for you and your family. Substitute nonfat frozen yogurt or sherbet for any craving for ice cream.

4. *Cheese*. Eliminate all cheeses on sandwiches. Do not eat chunk cheeses as a snack. Try to avoid these foods: French onion soup, pizza, and cheese dips.

Substitution food. Change eating habits to avoid all cheeses, but if cheese is to be used in cooking, use lite cheese.

5. *Butter*. Don't put butter on your food or cook with it. Butter is full of both cholesterol and saturated fats. The first habit to break is putting butter on your roll at a restaurant while waiting for your meal.

Substitution food. Margarine has no cholesterol but does contain saturated fats in varying degrees. The first ingredient on the label should be liquid safflower oil, liquid sunflower oil, or liquid corn oil. The hydrogenation process is necessary to solidify the margarine; the more hydrogenation, the greater the saturated fats. Therefore, "partially hydrogenated" may appear on the label but should not be the first listed. The softer, tub margarines contain less saturated fats.

One-Day Typical Diet

Breakfast: Bran cereal, topped with fruit, using
                 1 percent milk

Lunch: ½ Breast of chicken sandwich
                 Salad—vegetable with lite dressing
                 (or baked potato with vegetable toppings)
                 Diet drink or unsweetened tea

Dinner: Red snapper—broiled with lemon juice
                 Wild rice with mushrooms
                 French peas
                 Fresh raw vegetables—carrots, cauliflower,
                     radishes, etc.

Evening Snack: Popcorn (air-popped)
                 (or fruit)
                 Diet liquids

Exercise and Cholesterol

The role of exercise in controlling cholesterol has not been universally accepted from a medical standpoint, but there are significant statistics showing a direct relationship between a consistent exercise program and a decrease in coronary heart disease. The most concise information comes from a report by the Centers for Disease Control.

Exercise Decreases Risk of Coronary Heart Disease

This report revealed a statistically significant inverse association of exercise and coronary heart disease. It showed that exercise can decrease the likelihood of coronary heart diease.

The Common Causes of Heart Disease

The three most common causes of coronary heart disease are the following:

1. High cholesterol
2. High blood pressure
3. Cigarette smoking

When lack of exercise was compared to these three risk factors, it was found to be of similar magnitude in relationship to developing coronary heart disease.

RISK	RISK RATIO FOR DEVELOPING CORONARY HEART DISEASE
Smoking	2.50
High cholesterol	2.40
High blood pressure	2.10
Lack of exercise	1.90

Approximately 82 percent of Americans do not smoke. Many would not think of smoking a cigarette because it would be harmful to their health; yet they remain sedentary. Lack of exercise produces similar risks of developing coronary heart disease as do high cholesterol, smoking, and high blood pressure.

One possible cause for a decrease in coronary heart disease with exercise is an increase in "good" HDL-cholesterol in individuals who have a sustained exercise program lasting approximately thirty minutes a day, five days a week, equivalent to walking or jogging three miles a day. Overwhelming evidence indicates that physical activity does help prevent coronary heart disease.

EXERCISE PROGRAM
AFTER CHECKUP AND APPROVAL
BY YOUR PHYSICIAN

Frequency: Daily plan with five times a week minimum
Duration: 3-mile walk, jog, or equivalent (See "Duration Chart" below.)
            300 calories utilized per exercise session
            100 calories utilized per mile walked or jogged
Intensity: 75 percent maximum exercise capacity as determined by heart rate (See "Exercise Intensity Determination" below.)

Exercise Intensity Determination
(Based on heart rate)

> 220
> Minus age
> times 75 percent

Example: 40-year-old individual

> 220
> $- \ 40$
> 180
> $\times .75$
> 135 beats per minute as goal for sustained exercise

Duration Chart of Exercise Equivalences
Approximating 300 Calories
(Based on caloric use of 100 per mile of jogging or walking)

> Duration: 30 minutes
> Racquetball

Squash
Handball
Skiing, cross-country
Jogging, 10-minute mile
Bicycling, 12 mph
Swimming, freestyle, aggressive

Duration: 60 minutes
Bicycling, 5 mph
Calisthenics
Skating
Tennis
Volleyball, aggressive
Walking, 3 mph
Badminton

OAT BRAN AND CHOLESTEROL

Recent reports in the *Journal of the American Medical Association* and the *American Journal of Cardiology* point toward the beneficial effects of oat bran in lowering your cholesterol to the 20 percent range. Many individuals felt this was a panacea for controlling their cholesterol and relied only on oat bran for lowering elevated cholesterol. But it is not a magic solution to the cholesterol problem. The recommended amount of oat bran to eat is 50 to 100 grams or three to six bran muffins per day. Rolled oats or oatmeal with the whole oat grain consists of approximately one-half oat bran.

What Is Oat Bran?

The bran part of oat grain is the outer covering and is the source of the fiber so important in helping eliminate cholesterol from our bodies. The exact mechanism of the cholesterol-lowering process is not completely known, but it is felt that it acts as a resin that binds bile acids in the intestines and causes them to be excreted in the stool. These bile acids are formed from cholesterol in the liver; thus, more cholesterol is utilized and excreted from the body resulting in a lowering of the blood-cholesterol.

Many oat products available include the bran portion of the grain: rolled oats, oat flour, steel-cut oats, and quick rolled oats. Pure oat bran is the most concentrated form of the water-soluble fiber desired for lowering cholesterol.

The Big Picture of Cholesterol Control

In the body, there is a fine balance that has to be constantly kept in check to control the cholesterol level. In this regard, oat bran has received much emphasis, but proper eating habits have to be developed to ensure such control for lifetime effects. Diet, not oat bran, is the cornerstone for cholesterol control, and if we are to plan for the future health of our bodies, we must become aware of which foods are high in cholesterol and saturated fats. We must decide to eat less overall fat in our diets. We must change our present eating habits—from breakfast to evening snacks. We will have to take exercise seriously.

We Americans have to look squarely at other risk factors that play a role in heart attacks along with cholesterol: smoking, hypertension, obesity, family history of early heart attacks, diabetes, other arteries in our bodies showing signs of blockage, specifically low HDL-cholesterol counts. Being male is considered a risk factor for coronary heart disease.

We must take a good look at our eating life-style and determine that we must change what we have been eating for years and develop eating habits we can rely on for the rest of our lives. There is no one food we can start eating to combat the most serious enemy we will ever face in our lives. No one medication will protect us from so many different attacks on our arteries from so many different foods.

We must set goals to get our bodies into the best possible condition to prevent the silent killer from slowly and meticulously building up plaque that plugs the arteries vital to supplying blood to our hearts.

THE ROLE OF FIBER IN YOUR DIET

Two types of fiber are important in your diet.

1. Water-soluble fiber plays a role in lowering your cholesterol. Oat bran and beans are the two most common sources of water-soluble fiber.

2. Insoluble fiber has a significant effect in providing bulk in your stool and decreasing the time it takes for food to pass through your system. The National Cancer Institute recommends 25 to 35 grams of total fiber a day. It has been noted in populations with a high level of insoluble fiber in their diet that cancer of the colon, diverticulitis, diverticulosis, appendicitis, and hemorrhoids are markedly reduced or eliminated.

Wheat bran is the most common source of insoluble fiber, but corn bran, most fruits and vegetables, cereals, whole wheat breads, and popcorn are also included in this category.

TRACKING A BITE OF CHOLESTEROL

1. A breakfast of bacon and cheese omelette, buttered toast, and whole milk is eaten.

2. The cholesterol and saturated fats are digested and mixed with cholesterol manufactured by the liver.

3. The cholesterol is enveloped by protein, making it soluble in blood. The cholesterol is transported to body tissue.

4. About 60 to 90 percent of your transported cholesterol was produced by your liver, but the remaining portion came from what you ate. Eating too much cholesterol or saturated fat results in an excess of cholesterol in your blood.

5. Most of your cholesterol is carried in your blood as LDL-cholesterol (low-density lipoprotein-cholesterol). Excess LDL-cholesterol from your average American diet triggers the formation of plaque in your artery walls, which continues to build up until it blocks the flow of blood in those arteries.

6. HDL-cholesterol is a small portion of the cholesterol-protein packet traveling in the blood. This high-density lipoprotein-cholesterol acts as a scavenger, removing excess cholesterol from the blood, and probably from the artery wall plaque as well.

7. The excess cholesterol is then carried to the liver for disposal along with excess LDL-cholesterol traveling in the blood.

8. The only process known to eliminate cholesterol from the body is through the manufacture of bile by the liver, cholesterol being the precursor of bile. Cholesterol and bile acids are thus eliminated into the intestines where a portion is reabsorbed by the intestines and a portion is eliminated in the stool.

9. Certain cholesterol-lowering drugs, as well as oat bran, bind these cholesterol-rich bile acids in the intestines, prohibiting them from being reabsorbed, eliminating them in the stool. The result: a lower total amount of cholesterol in the body.

10. Other cholesterol-lowering drugs can lower the body's cholesterol level by inhibiting the production of cholesterol by the liver.

11. A double cheeseburger and chocolate milk shake are eaten for lunch with a small ice-cream cone for dessert.

12. *Recycle another bite of cholesterol.*

DIETARY RECOMMENDATIONS

The American Heart Association says to consume no more than 300 mg of cholesterol daily. Cholesterol is found in foods of animal origin, such as meat, eggs, and dairy products. Consume 50 percent of your calories as carbohydrates, 20 percent as protein, and 30 percent as fat with less than 10 percent of fat calories from saturated fat (found in all foods of animal origin and in coconut, palm, and palm kernel oils as well as cocoa butter). Up to 10 percent of fat calories may come from polyunsaturated fats (found in fish, canola, safflower, sunflower, corn, soybean, and cottonseed oils; they are liquid at room temperature). The remaining fat calories come from monounsaturated fat sources (olives, olive oil, peanuts, peanut oil, peanut butter, and avocados).

THE SAVE YOUR LIFE
CHOLESTEROL PLAN

1. Total Calories

Obesity in itself is associated with an elevated LDL-cholesterol; it is also an independent risk factor of coronary heart disease. Weight reduction will lower LDL-cholesterol in many people, and reducing to a normal body weight may completely correct an elevated cholesterol level. Check what your desirable body weight should be and set your goal to get there. This step cannot be emphasized strongly enough!

It is difficult to know and develop accurate percentages of the foods you eat. Adopt eating habits that will ensure fewer saturated fats and cholesterol and more complex carbohydrates. Choose the majority of your foods from the vegetable, grain, and fruit categories, which will satisfy your hunger. Eat less meat, especially red meat. Avoid fats of any kind, eliminating as much fried food as possible.

2. Cholesterol

Especially high sources of cholesterol are egg yolks and organ meats (liver, brain, sweetbread). Beef, pork, lamb, chicken, and fish all contain some cholesterol. Dairy products—whole milk, butter, and cheese—contain cholesterol. Concentrate on those foods with lower cholesterol levels on a daily basis.

3. Meats

Beef, veal, pork, and lamb contain more cholesterol-saturated fat combination than chicken, turkey, and fish. Use only lean cuts, and trim all visible fat from the outside before cooking. Substitute beans, peas, pasta, rice, breads, and cereals. These are high in both carbohydrates and protein and can be used in large amounts with small amounts of meat to ensure adequate protein with less fat and total calories.

4. Chicken and Turkey

The skin of poultry should be removed due to the layer of fat just beneath the skin. Decrease intake of beef, pork, and lamb while substituting portions of poultry. Poultry does not contain as much absorbable iron as beef, pork, and lamb. Do not cancel the good effect of chicken's and turkey's lower saturated fat and cholesterol by frying the meat in cooking oils high in saturated fat or by using sauces rich in fat.

5. Processed Meats

These contain large amounts of fats. Decrease or virtually eliminate eating bologna, salami, hot dogs, and sausage.

6. Fish

Fish is lower than beef, lamb, and pork in cholesterol and is low in saturated fat. Don't fry it in cooking oils high in saturated fats. Bathe in lemon juice rather than cholesterol-laden sauces.

7. Shellfish

Most kinds of shellfish contain less fat than red meat and poultry, but their cholesterol content varies. Shrimp contains the most, scallops the least.

8. Dairy Products

Use skim milk or 1 percent milk, which is a good source of calcium. Avoid natural and processed cheese; use only limited amounts of imitation or lite cheeses. Buy cheese with the lowest grams of fat shown on the label.

Here are some other dairy products ranked according to percentage of fat:

PRODUCT	APPROXIMATE PERCENTAGE OF FAT
Yogurt	1
Sherbet	2

Ice milk	4
Whole milk	4
Ice cream	10
Half and Half	12
Cream	20
Natural cheeses	35
Whipping cream	40
Cream cheese	40

9. Eggs

Eliminate known eggs from your diet. Egg yolks are often hidden in cooking, making it difficult to know how many eggs you are eating in a week's time. One egg yolk contains about 275 mg of cholesterol. Egg whites contain no cholesterol. Use two egg whites or commercial egg substitutes in place of one egg required in a recipe.

10. Cooking Fats and Oils

AVOID	USE
Animal fats and oils	Canola oil
Deep frying	Safflower oil
Lard	Cottonseed oil
Coconut oil	Olive oil
Palm oil	Corn oil
Palm kernel oil	Sunflower oil
Butter	Soybean oil

Canola oil has the lowest saturated fat content of all vegetable oils. Safflower oil is high in "good" polyunsaturated fat and low in "bad" saturated fat.

11. Fiber

Eat fruit three times a day. Eat whole pieces of fruit rather than drink the juices in order to obtain the added fiber. Eat the membranes of fruit for the same reason.

Choose bran-type cereals. Add three to four teaspoons of whole bran to 40 percent bran cereals.

Add as many vegetables to your daily diet as possible. Make them a significant part of each meal.

12. Saturated Fats (Fatty Acids)

Saturated fats cause an elevation of your blood-cholesterol and should be considered in the same category as cholesterol. Some foods are advertised as low in cholesterol, but they are high in saturated fat. Saturated fatty acids are not needed in the diet at all.

SOURCES HIGH IN SATURATED FAT

ANIMAL ORIGIN	PLANT ORIGIN
Beef	Cocoa butter (chocolate)
Butter	Coconut oil
Cheese	Palm kernel oil
Cream	Palm oil
Ice cream	
Lamb	
Pork	
Whole milk	

13. Monounsaturated Fats (Fatty Acids)

Recent evidence shows these may cause a decrease in LDL-cholesterol when used instead of saturated fatty acids: olive oil; canola oil (rapeseed); sunflower seed oil (some forms); and safflower oil (some forms).

14. Polyunsaturated Fats (Fatty Acids)

These are mainly vegetable in origin, but the fat in fish is polyunsaturated. They can produce a cholesterol-lowering effect in the blood but are not recommended to be used in excess because they are high in total calories. Polyunsaturated fats of *vegetable origin* (omega-6 fatty acids) include safflower oil, sunflower oil, corn oil, and soybean oil.

There has been little documentation that omega-3 fatty acids (polyunsaturated fats of *fish origin*) actually reduce LDL-cholesterol in your blood. There has been some evidence that eating fish does have the effect of reducing the risk of developing coronary heart disease. This finding may be independent of omega-3 fatty acids. For these reasons, fish oil supplements are not recommended.

15. Alcohol

Reports conflict as to alcohol's effect on coronary heart disease. A large consumption of alcohol is proven to have an adverse effect on health. Alcohol does not affect LDL-cholesterol; it does cause a rise in HDL-cholesterol but may be a fraction of HDL-cholesterol that offers no protection against coronary heart disease. The use of alcohol for protection from coronary heart disease is not recommended.

16. Nuts

Nuts are high in fats with associated high calories. Most nuts contain mainly unsaturated fats. The largest problem with nuts lies in their high caloric content.

17. Best Cooking Methods

Steaming, broiling, grilling, stir-frying, and baking are recommended. The advent of microwave ovens has made it easier and more efficient to do certain kinds of cooking. Using PAM or other vegetable sprays eliminates the need to grease pans with harmful oils; also, nonstick pans are good in this regard. Choose a liquid vegetable oil when you have to use a cooking oil, don't use butter or animal fat in cooking. No longer rely on frying as a cooking method in your kitchen.

APPENDIX C

CHILDREN AND CHOLESTEROL

One hundred and five young American soldiers killed in action in Vietnam were the subjects of a study concerned with blockage in the coronary arteries. The mean age of the subjects was 22.1 years. Forty-five percent had some degree of atherosclerosis in one or more of their coronary arteries. Twenty-five percent had involvement of at least two of the three main arteries of the heart.

When did these blockages begin? There seems to be no doubt that cholesterol buildup starts early in life, but there is evidence that the process is reversible if intervention is effected before the formations of plaque advances and matures. Dr. Robert Jones, cardiac surgeon at Duke, states that this process begins in the teenage years; others report that it begins even earlier.

WHEN THE CHOLESTEROL PROCESS BEGINS

An article in *Pediatrics* submitted by the Louisiana State University Medical Center stated that fatty streaks of atherosclerosis begin in childhood and that both fatty streaks and fibrous plaques appear in the coronary arteries during the second decade of life. These streaks and plaques were correlated with levels of fats and cholesterol in the blood of children and adolescents.

Another article in *Pediatrics* involved youngsters ages eight to eighteen when first studied and ages twenty to thirty when reexamined more than ten years later. That study indicated that elevated levels of cholesterol during childhood were associated with a higher risk for elevation in adult life. Total cholesterol measurements in childhood were shown to be predictors of adult LDL-cholesterol levels, with twenty-five percent to fifty percent of adult cholesterol variability explained by childhood levels.

HIGH CHOLESTEROL AND HIGH RATE OF CORONARY DISEASE

One other report showed the cholesterol levels of children were found to be lowest in countries where incidence of coronary heart disease is also low; levels were found to be highest in countries where incidence of coronary heart disease is the highest. Cholesterol levels of children in the United States were found in the latter group.

Many pediatricians do not feel comfortable limiting cholesterol in the diet of growing children. They cite the need for cholesterol in building cell walls, hormones, and nerve structures. The American Academy of Pediatrics' Committee on Nutrition reported that children with family histories of either early coronary heart disease or elevated cholesterol should have a complete evaluation of their cholesterol, other lipids, and lipoproteins. The committee does not favor testing all school children as a part of routine checkups for various reasons.

There have been no extensive studies showing the effects of a low cholesterol diet on the maturation of young people or the effects of such a diet in relation to coronary heart disease. Such studies would be difficult and are probably not forthcoming.

TEACH YOUR CHILDREN

The questions remain: When did the blockages begin in those young Americans killed in Vietnam? And what can be done to prevent early buildup of atheromatous plaque in the arteries of the heart?

There is no clear consensus on how to diagnose which children have high cholesterol; nor is there consensus on how aggressive we should be in preventing children from eating cholesterol and saturated fats. One thing is clear, however. Eating habits are formed to a great degree during childhood and adolescence. Habits of diet, exercise, weight control, and often smoking are all established in childhood and carry over into adulthood. Once such habits are formed, they are changed only with great difficulty in the adult.

We should teach our children about cholesterol and saturated fats and help them to develop good eating habits at a young age. If the attempts to lower the cholesterol of the general American population are to be effective, the eating habits of the entire family must be changed.

Our children should be taught the physiology of cholesterol in the body, taught which foods are high in cholesterol and saturated fats, and made to cut down on the excess of those foods eaten in abundance by the youth of America. Some moderation has to be taught. Children can follow a nutritious diet, with adequate calories and protein for growth and development, yet still reduce the amount of fat they eat in fried foods and bakery products.

A serum cholesterol should be obtained for your child if you have any family history of high blood-cholesterol or of heart attack before age fifty-five. The decision whether your child should have a cholesterol drawn rests with you in conjunction with your child's pediatrician.

Educate your children on cholesterol and saturated fats. Teach them proper eating habits related to cholesterol and saturated fats versus complex carbohydrates. What they learn now will carry over with them into adulthood and may determine whether your children become coronary artery statistics.

242